CULTURES OF THE WORLD®

RUSSIA

Oleg Torchinsky / Angela Black

BENCHMARK BOOKS

MARSHALL CAVENDISH
NEW YORK

PICTURE CREDITS
Cover photo: © Peter Arnold, Inc.: Bilderberg © Ernsting
alt.TYPE/REUTERS: 111 • ANA Press Agency: 6, 18 • Bes Stock: 40, 70, 80 • Kenny Chan/China Tourism
Photo Library: 71, 78, 106 • Focus Team Italy: 46, 61, 86, 108 • HBL Network Photo Agency: 56, 57, 58,
59, 64, 85 • Dave G. Houser/Houserstock: 94 • Hulton-Deutsch Collection: 31, 44 • Hutchison Library: 7,
17, 53, 66, 82, 83, 84, 96, 105 • Image Bank: 4, 13, 35, 39, 42, 49, 88 • Victoria Ivleva-Yorke/Hutchison
Library: 54 • Bjorn Klingwall: 8, 50, 112 • Life File Photographic Library: 3, 15, 68, 72, 75, 76, 79, 81,
87, 93, 110, 113, 119, 121 • Buddy Mays Travel Stock Photography: 5, 62 • Terence Nottingham /Eye
Ubiquitous: 60 • Russian Information Agency *Novosti*: 10, 11 (both) 16, 20, 23, 24, 26, 27, 28, 29, 30, 32,
33, 34, 36, 37, 38, 51, 52, 65, 67 (both), 73, 77, 89, 92, 99, 100, 102, 103, 118, 125, 126, 128, 129 • Bernard
Sonnerville: 115, 116 • STOCKFOOD/DAROTA I BOGDAN BIALY: 130 • STOCKFOOD/KARL NEWEDEL:
131 • Liba Taylor: 14, 91, 109, 117, 122, 124, 127 • Anatoly Tchezey/Hutchison Library: 55 • Audrius
Tomonis/www.banknotes.com: 135 • TopFoto: 114, 120

ACKNOWLEDGMENTS
Thanks to Valentina G. Brougher, Professor of Languages and Linguistics at Georgetown University
for her expert reading of this manuscript.

PRECEDING PAGE
Russians who live in the rural parts of the country have their own local festivities where they celebrate
with song.

Marshall Cavendish Benchmark
99 White Plains Road
Tarrytown, NY 10591
Website: www.marshallcavendish.us

Originated and designed by Times Editions
An imprint of Marshall Cavendish International (Asia) Private Limited,
A member of the Times Publishing Group

Library of Congress Cataloging-in-Publication Data
Torchinsky, O. (Oleg)
  Russia / by Oleg Torchinsky.
    p. cm. — (Cultures of the world)
  Summary: "Explores the geography, history, government, economy, people, and culture
    of Russia"—Provided by publisher.
  Includes bibliographical references and index.
  ISBN 0-7614-1849-0
  1. Russia (Federation)—Juvenile literature. I. Title. II. Cultures of the world (2nd ed.).
  DK510.23.T67 2005
  947—dc22   2004027512

Printed in China

7 6 5 4 3 2 1

CONTENTS

Reindeer racing is popular in Russia's frozen north.

A Russian girl looks out of her wooden playhouse.

INTRODUCTION

In 1991, after 73 years of Communist rule, the United Soviet Socialist Republic (USSR) ceased to exist and a new country was born—the Russian Federation.

The Russian Federation is the largest country in the world. It borders 14 countries, straddles two continents, and accommodates 11 time zones. Its rich and fascinating history, as well as its remarkable cultural contributions, are admired throughout the Western world.

Russians have contributed some of the finest works of art and architecture, literature, music, and dance. Russia was the first country to reach outer space. It also made significant scientific achievements in chemistry, psychology, aerodynamics, and engineering.

Within Russia's boundless expanses, Western and Eastern civilizations have converged and mixed to produce a rich and remarkable culture. At the dawning of the 21st century, a modern country has emerged, taking steps toward democracy.

GEOGRAPHY

THE RUSSIAN FEDERATION, which covers almost one-eighth of the world's land area and is about 1.8 times the size of the United States, is the world's largest country, stretching for more than 5,600 miles (9,000 km) from east to west, and 2,500 miles (4,025 km) from north to south. It occupies most of eastern Europe and almost all of northern Asia. The border between the two great continents—Europe and Asia—runs through its boundless expanses. A monument has been erected where this border is calculated to be; tourists like to be photographed there, standing with one foot in Europe and the other in Asia. Russia's landscape includes almost every geographical feature imaginable.

PLAINS AND MOUNTAINS

In the west of Russia there are huge plains stretching thousands of miles that are called the Russian (or East European) Lowland; the Ural Mountains separate this area from another huge lowland—the West Siberian Plain. The southwest of Russia ends in the high ranges of the Caucasus Mountains, where Mount Elbrus at 18,481 feet (5,633 m) is the country's highest peak.

In the east of the country is the Central Siberian Plateau, and if you travel farther east you will reach the mountainous regions of southern and northeastern Siberia and the Far East.

Russia is a great marine power. In the north it is washed by the Arctic Ocean and in the east by the Pacific Ocean. Through St. Petersburg it has

Above: **Sheep cling to the mountainside in the Dagestan Republic, which is located in the Caucasus Mountains.**

Opposite: **A Russian bear roams the wilds of Russia with the majestic Kamchatka volcano rising behind.**

7

Trading vessels moor on the Volga River at Nizhniy Novgorod, formerly called Gorky, after the city's most famous son, Maxim Gorky, the writer and revolutionary.

an outlet to the Baltic Sea, and thus also to the Atlantic Ocean. Russia's ships can reach the Mediterranean through the Black Sea.

RIVERS AND LAKES

Russia has many great rivers. One of the greatest is the Volga River, which is one of Russia's national symbols. Although the Volga is not Russia's longest river, there is no other river about which as many songs and books have been written. The Volga has been known since ancient times, when it was called *Ra;* in the Middle Ages, it was known as *Itil.* Beginning in the depths of Russia as a tiny spring, the Volga flows south, becoming ever wider and stronger. After 2,193 miles (3,530 km) it forms a broad delta and flows into the Caspian Sea. A small chapel has been built at the source of the Volga.

But the mighty Volga cannot compete with the huge and powerful rivers of Siberia—the Ob, Lena, Yenisey, and Angara. They are each so wide that if you stand on one bank you cannot see the opposite side.

LAKE BAIKAL Among Russia's thousands of lakes, one is unique— Lake Baikal, the world's largest freshwater basin. At 5,315 feet (1,620 m) and 25 million years old, it is the deepest and oldest lake in the world. It is the habitat of a variety of flora and fauna (1,800 types), including some that are found nowhere else in the world. Another interesting feature distinguishes Baikal from other lakes: 336 rivers flow into the lake, while there is only one outlet, the lower Angara River.

CLIMATE AND SEASONS

Due to its large size, Russia has a variety of different climatic conditions, according to region and the time of year. In the northern arctic and subarctic zones, the average winter temperature is –58°F (–50°C). By contrast, in the south and the Caucasus, summer temperatures can reach 110°F (43°C). Western Russia has a typical continental climate, with hot summers of up to 86°F (30°C) and cold winters as low as –13°F (–25°C).

The Russian year is clearly divided into four seasons that sharply differ from each other: winter, spring, summer, and fall. The winter months of December, January, and February have frosts, ice, and snowstorms. During this season, the earth is blanketed in white snow and ice. Before the winter comes, birds migrate to warmer lands, insects hide in the tree bark or go underground, and animals find shelter in dens and lairs.

Spring in western Russia begins in March and lasts through April and May. This is the time when the first flowers appear from under the snow; they are called snowdrops. The ice on the rivers begins to melt and break up, turning into rivulets of water. Rooks are the first birds to return from faraway countries, announcing the arrival of spring.

Spring is followed by the summer months: June, July, and August. Everything blooms; everything thrives and bears fruit.

Fall is considered the most beautiful time of the year. It is called "golden autumn," because the forest leaves turn golden-red. Particularly beautiful are the maple trees, whose leaves acquire a golden and bright-red tinge. In November, the trees shed their leaves, with only their bare branches outlined in black in the forest. Birds migrate southward to warmer lands, and animals hasten to hide in their warm dens.

The golomyanka, a type of fish from the bullhead family, is found only in Lake Baikal. This fish gives birth to live young. The Baikal or nerpa seal is the only mammal in the lake.

THE NORTH

The winter is particularly long in the north, where the land is washed by the Arctic Ocean. Much of this region is almost perpetually ice-bound. Somewhere in this region of ice and eternal frost is the North Pole.

But the North Pole is not the coldest spot on Earth. The coldest spot is a place called Oymyakon in Siberia. There, the temperature in winter may drop to −160°F (−106°C), a temperature that is hard to imagine. A bird that dares to fly out of its nest in such weather freezes and drops to the ground dead, frozen solid. On such days people stay home, and if they have to go outdoors, they wear clothes made of fur and cover their faces with special fur masks. They have to breathe through cloth or fur to prevent their lungs from freezing.

In the north, the winter lasts seven to eight months of the year. During this period it is dark and cold, with raging snowstorms and blizzards. The boundless tundra (vast, nearly treeless plains) is blanketed with snow; the bare forests and the cold empty plains are a terrible and unusual sight. But there is a strange phenomenon doctors and psychologists call the "disease of the north." People who have spent some time in the north often want to return there. Neither the warm sea nor palms attract them; all they want is to go back to the cold regions of ice and snow.

One of the most magnificent sights in this part of the world is the Northern Lights. The effect of this strange phenomenon is as if someone were showing a color movie across the sky, with gold, white, silvery, bluish, pink, yellow, and red streamers and bands moving in ripples and illuminating the dark winter sky. This enchanting sight lasts one or two hours, gradually fading away until the sky sinks back into darkness. If you are lucky enough to see the Northern Lights, you will never forget the sight. The mechanism that causes this magnificent display is not fully understood, but it is connected with the proximity of the magnetic North Pole to high solar winds.

Opposite, top: **Hares inhabit Russia's central plains and grasslands.**

Opposite, bottom: **A polar bear in Russia's northern arctic wastes.**

FAUNA

An extremely large variety of animal, bird, reptile, and insect species live in Russia. Thousands of different fishes and marine animals inhabit its waters, and thousands of different plants and trees grow in its forests.

The main animals inhabiting the forests of western Russia include the brown bear, wolf, fox, hare, hedgehog, and polecat; and among the most common birds are the wood grouse, black grouse, partridge, hazel grouse, crow, magpie, and sparrow.

Other animals include the polar bear, which lives in the north among the snow and ice; the walrus; and the reindeer. Aurochs, a very ancient form of cattle dating back to the Ice Ages, nearly became extinct in recent times. It took conservationists much effort to find several animals and gradually revive the Russian herd. The Siberian *taiga* (TAI-gah) or subarctic forest, is also the habitat of sables; their fur is so beautiful and soft that it is often called "soft gold." In the Far Eastern *taiga,* there still roam a small number of Siberian tigers, which are an endangered species.

Russia's bird and insect species are much like those found in other regions of the world north of the equator. Many of the birds migrate to southern Asia for the winter months. Russian butterflies are very large but not as bright as their tropical counterparts. Their coloring is designed to blend with the vegetation of Russia's middle belt—its fields, meadows, flowers, and grasses.

FLORA

In Russia forests cover vast areas of land, particularly in Siberia, where they sometimes stretch for hundreds or thousands of miles. The trees in Russian forests are of the coniferous and deciduous varieties. The coniferous trees include firs, pines, larches, and cedars—all of which are majestic and beautiful with needle-like leaves and a

THE BEAR AND THE EAGLE

The brown bear is Russia's national animal and adorns many city and family coats of arms. Evidently the distant forefathers of the Russians and other Slavic nations deified this powerful and beautiful animal, often calling it the Master of Forests. They worshipped the animal and offered sacrifices to it; if they did hunt bears, it was only for the purpose of testing themselves against the bear's strength and courage.

In the ancient past, as people hunted, they never said the word for "bear" out loud because they believed that animals could understand human speech and thus would be forewarned. Instead, people used various descriptive phrases. One of these phrases probably accounts for the word "bear" in Russian: *medved* (mid-VYED), which literally means "one who knows where the honey is."

The double-headed eagle is the state symbol of Russia and first appeared in the country in the 15th century. Initially the insignia of the Byzantium dynasty, the emblem was brought over into Russia when Sophia Paleolog, a princess of the last imperial Byzantium family, married the Great Duke of Moscow, Ivan III. For four centuries, the two-headed eagle remained an emblem for Russia until the 1917 Revolution. It was reinstated as the state symbol by President Boris Yeltsin in November 1993.

Through the ages, many meanings have been attributed to the symbol. The most common explanation is that the two heads represent the two parts of Russia—the part in Europe and the part in Asia—and both are equally important.

wonderful resinous smell. Russians bring fir trees into their homes and decorate them with glistening ornaments and lights at Christmas time. The deciduous trees growing in Russia include the aspen, oak, maple, poplar, and ash.

The tree that is particularly loved by Russians is the birch. Its slender branches, smooth white bark, and small bright-green leaves that quiver in the wind have always inspired artists and poets to compare it to a graceful young girl. In pagan times, people paid homage to the birch, decorating it with bright ribbons, flowers, and gifts. The birch was also held in high esteem for other reasons: it made good fuel; its bark could be used for weaving *lapti* (LAP-ti), which are very light and comfortable bark shoes, and also for making special baskets for berries and mushrooms. In ancient times, before paper was invented, Russians wrote letters, notes, and official documents on birch bark.

CITIES: MOSCOW AND ST. PETERSBURG

Moscow and St. Petersburg are perceived by many Russians as Russia's twin capitals; for many centuries the cities have competed with each other to hold the dominant position as Russia's center.

MOSCOW Moscow, the officially recognized capital of the Russian Federation, is one of Russia's oldest cities; it was first mentioned in chronicles back in 1147. It has played a major role in unifying the Russian lands into a single powerful state. In the 14th century, Moscow became the central point around which the feuding Russian principalities began to unify. It was in Moscow that the Kievan Grand Duke had his headquarters, which served as a fortress for him and his troops. The town began to grow around the fortress, called the Kremlin. It is interesting to note that the medieval Kremlin fortress remains the political and administrative center of the city and of all of Russia. This is the seat of Russia's government, and where the president receives foreign guests.

An old woman walks past a carpet of flowers in the small town of Zagorsk near Moscow.

The city has developed around the Kremlin and the adjacent massive Red Square, which is Moscow's main square. With a population of around 11 million, Moscow is one of the world's largest cities. It is a large industrial center, with major machine-building and instrument-making plants, steel works, and a large number of factories. It is also a major cultural center with dozens of theaters, cinemas, art galleries, museums, and stadiums.

Modern Moscow consists of glass and concrete high-rise office buildings and hotels similar to those of any other city in the world. Moscow also has a great number of historical monuments and fine examples of old churches, palaces, and grand houses of differing styles, which give the city enormous character.

Moscow cityscape. In the foreground is the Bell Tower of Ivan the Great, built between 1505 and 1508. At 266 feet (81 m) it is the highest structure in the Kremlin fortress. In contrast, Moscow's many modern apartment blocks can be seen in the background.

ST. PETERSBURG

ST. PETERSBURG St. Petersburg is a symbol of modern Russia. From 1924 until 1991, it was known as Leningrad, named after the leader of the Soviet revolution, Vladimir Ilyich Lenin (1870–1924). Moscow is a bustling, picturesque city that has developed over the course of centuries, unplanned, with streets clustering together at random. By contrast, St. Petersburg is a European-style city designed and built according to a specific plan. It is a city of long straight avenues and regularly contoured squares.

On May 16, 1703, Tsar Peter I ordered the city to be built on a site he had selected. He conceived this as the new capital of Russia, intending it to play an important role in European life, as well as open a door to the West. He named the city St. Petersburg in honor of his patron saint. The construction of the city was extremely difficult, with significant loss of life, since it was built on marshlands. Peter employed Europe's and Russia's best architects, and today St. Petersburg is one of the great cities of the world.

St. Petersburg is Russia's second largest industrial and cultural center (after Moscow), and its second, northern capital. Its population now numbers around 4 million. The city has a large number of beautiful historical palaces, squares, and streets. Its magnificent historical sites—the Winter Palace, Dvortsovaya (Palace) Square, the Admiralty, Saint Isaac's Cathedral, and the Russian Museum—have been listed by UNESCO as among the greatest treasures of world culture.

Snow thaws around Dvortsovaya Square in St. Petersburg. In the background is the Winter Palace, so called because it was the former winter residence of the Russian tsars. It is now known as the Hermitage Museum, one of the largest buildings of its kind in the world.

OTHER REGIONS

There are several other cities and towns of historical significance in western Russia. Among them are Novgorod and Pskov, which before the 16th century were independent city-states ruled by the boyars, as well as Vladimir, Tver, Yaroslavl, Ryazan, Smolensk, and Kostroma.

Going eastward, there are many other significant towns. For example, the Volga has always been a well settled region, because it provided settlers with fertile land as well as served as an extremely convenient transportation artery for carrying cargo and people to the north. Nizhniy Novgorod, situated on the Volga, became a major trading center whose fairs won fame worldwide. In the 17th century, a chain of fortresses were built along the Volga River in order to hold back the intrusions of hordes of nomads from the south and east. These fortresses became the towns of Simbirsk (now Ulyanovsk), Samara, Saratov, and Tsarytsin (now Volgograd). When invasions no longer threatened, the fortresses turned into prospering commercial centers.

A reindeer breeder's camp out on the vast northern tundra.

Kazan, a Tatar city and former capital of the Kazan Khannate, stands by itself. Though conquered in the 16th century, it has preserved its Islamic features and is now the capital of Tatarstan.

Beyond the Volga are the vast dry steppes (plains), followed by the Ural Mountains, which abound in minerals and precious and semiprecious stones, and are a major industrial region of Russia. This region began to develop rapidly at the beginning of the 18th century. The cities of this region are Chelyabinsk, Yekaterinburg, Magnitogorsk, and Perm.

Siberia's chief towns are situated in its southern regions along the giant Trans-Siberian railway: Irkutsk, Omsk, Tomsk, and Novosibirsk. These towns were built by rich industrialists. The houses there are strong, warm, spacious, and functional. These towns have many beautiful palaces and churches, and theaters built in the classical style. Russia's Far East has its own capital cities: Khabarovsk, Vladivostok, and Petropavlovsk-Kamchatskiy. For many years Vladivostok was a closed naval base, and for that reason foreigners were not allowed to visit it. Now it is open to everyone and is developing into a center for Russian-Chinese trade.

HISTORY

RUSSIANS ACCOUNT for the bulk of the population of the Russian Federation. The Russians are Slavs. Slavic peoples are divided into Western, Southern, and Eastern Slavs. The Western Slavs are the Czechs, the Slovaks, and the Poles; the Southern are the Bulgarians, the Serbians, the Croats, and the Slovenes; and the Eastern Slavs are the Russians, the Ukrainians, and the Belarusians. In the first century A.D., the Eastern Slavs lived along the Dnieper River and around Lake Ilmen.

THE SLAVS

The first record of the Slavs has been found in works of fifth- and sixth-century Byzantine historians. According to these records, the Slavs were a handsome, tall, and strong people with fair hair; they were brave fighting men of great endurance, and hospitable hosts in peacetime. Their main occupation was farming. They sowed rye, wheat, barley, and millet, and traded, hunted, and fished. Beating off forays of aggressive Scandinavian Vikings from the north and nomads from the south, the individual principalities gradually formed a large state that was headed by the grand dukes of Kiev. This state came to be known as Kievan Rus. Kiev, now the capital of Ukraine, was located on the main trade route connecting the Baltic Sea with the Black Sea and the Byzantine Empire.

Kievan Rus established trade with the cities of Asia and Europe: Prague, Constantinople, and Baghdad. In the 10th century, warriors directed by the Kievan dukes Oleg, Igor, and Svyatoslav made raids on the richest and most powerful city at this time—Byzantium. In 911, after Duke Oleg and his large army besieged Constantinople, the Byzantines had to conclude a treaty with Russia, under which Russian merchants received the right to come to Tsargrad (as the Russians called Constantinople) and to trade there free of duty or tax.

It is mentioned in chronicles that the Kievan Duke Oleg nailed his shield to the gate of the Byzantine capital, Constantinople, as a token of victory.

Opposite: **The Bronze Horseman is a tribute to Peter the Great, one of the greatest rulers of Russia. It was commissioned by Catherine II in order to create a link between her and the great king. The inscription on the pedestal reads "Peter the First, Catherine the Second 1782" in Latin on one side, with a similar one in Russian on the other.**

A painting by artist Nikolai Roerich (1874–1947) called *Overseas Guests*, depicts Viking traders traveling along the Volga River in the ninth century.

The Russian social system gradually became feudal. As the economy developed, the peasants and craftsmen began to produce more products and goods. Surpluses appeared and the tribal nobility—the elders, military leaders, fighting men—appropriated them. Now they could live at the expense of the work done by peasants and craftsmen who depended on them. The princes seized common lands and gave only small plots to the peasants so that they could maintain themselves and their families by working for the landowners. The feudal lords were called boyars.

As the old Russian feudal state became larger and stronger, it began to establish diplomatic relations with other European countries. Orthodox Christianity in Byzantium attracted the Russians, as they thought Christianity glorified autocracy. Grand Prince Vladimir I became a Christian in 988 and made Christianity the official religion in Kievan Rus. The old idols of the heathen gods were thrown into the river. Orthodox priests, who came from Constantinople, christened the Russians in the water of the Dnieper River.

KIEVAN RUS AND THE MONGOL INVASION

Kievan Rus flourished in the 11th century during the rule of Grand Duke Yaroslav the Wise (1019–54). Under him, Russia became the largest European state—it stretched from the Gulf of Finland in the northwest, to the Black Sea coast and the lower Danube in the south, and from the Carpathian Mountains in the west, to the upper Volga in the east. Foreign kings sought to establish friendly relations with Kievan Rus. Yaroslav married a Swedish princess, and married his daughters to French, Hungarian, and Norwegian kings.

In the 13th century, Kievan Rus faced a severe challenge: the powerful Mongol state, with its capital in Karakorum, appeared in the heart of Central Asia. Genghis Khan, a clever, talented, and cruel man, was its powerful leader. He succeeded in creating an aggressive, well armed, disciplined, and mobile army. Within a short time, the Tatars (as the Mongols were known) had conquered Siberia, China, Central Asia, and the Caucasus. Kievan Rus was unable to withstand the invasion. In 1223 three uncoordinated Russian detachments were defeated on the banks of the Kalka River (now Kalmius), not far from the mouth of the Don River.

After Genghis Khan's death, the Tatars began their second wave of westward expansion. His grandson, Batu Khan, wanted to conquer the whole of Europe. Over the course of three years (1237–40), the Russians courageously defended their homeland: many cities were defended to the last man. By the end of the 1250s, the rule of the Tatar Khans was established in Kievan Rus.

THE RISE OF MOSCOW AND IVAN THE TERRIBLE

On returning from his European raid, Batu Khan and his court settled on the banks of the lower Volga, where the state of the Golden Horde was formed with its capital at Sarai. This foreign oppression brought innumerable calamities to Kievan Rus. The destruction of towns and the plundering of the country's riches set Russia's development back two centuries.

As the years passed, the country gradually began to recover from the destruction. Towns rose from ruins, becoming the first centers of the struggle for liberation. Moscow grew strong. The city became a great crafts and trading center in an advantageous position: it was at the crossing of

The fragmentation of Kievan Rus due to Mongol invasions led to the emergence of several regional centers. Two Russian towns achieved prominence: Novgorod (a powerful mercantile capital) and Moscow (a centrally located trading town). The Golden Horde held firmly to the steppes bordering the forest realms of the Russians. The grand princes of Moscow paid homage to the Mongols in exchange for protection in local feuds and conflicts. In this way the Muscovites gained increasing local power.

Under Ivan III, the double-headed eagle borrowed from Byzantium became the emblem of the Russian state. It symbolized Moscow's connection with the once powerful Byzantium.

trade routes and far from the outlying districts that were constantly threatened by enemy attacks. In the second half of the 14th century, after a leadership struggle, Khan Mamay consolidated the Golden Horde for some time. By then, Moscow had stopped carrying out the Khan's orders, so he decided to punish them. On September 8, 1380, Russians led by Grand Duke Dmitri Ivanovich met Mamay's army at Kulikovo Field near the Don River. The Russians won the fierce battle. A hundred years later, during the rule of Ivan III (1462–1505), known as Russia's unifier, the Tatars' power came to an end. In 1480 Ivan stopped paying taxes to the Tatars and established Russia's national independence. Under Ivan III's son, Vasily III (1505–33), all the princedoms and lands of Russia, without exception, were finally unified—some voluntarily, others by force. They formed a new state, bringing to an end the wasteful feudal wars. The economy and culture began to develop rapidly.

IVAN THE TERRIBLE Under the son of Vasily III, Ivan IV (1533–84), the state's power continued to grow stronger and some changes occurred within the class of feudal lords. Along with the rich landowners, the boyars, there appeared a social group of small landowners—the gentry. They received land from the boyars in return for military service. This social group was later destined to become Russia's dominant social class.

Under the rule of Ivan IV, the first ruler to be crowned tsar, the Kazan and Astrakhan khanates were conquered (in 1552 and 1556), and as a result the Volga region became Russian, as did western Siberia and the Urals.

Ivan's reign went down in history as one of the most bloody. He instituted a system of terror, *oprichnina* (ah-PRICH-ni-na), directed against both the boyars and the common people. Groups of black-clad *oprichnics* broke into houses, killing and robbing both old and young, and committing other excesses. Because of the *oprichnina* and other actions, he became known as Ivan the Terrible.

Following the death of Ivan the Terrible there was a period known as the Time of Troubles, when anarchy and instability reigned, one tsar often quickly replacing another. Taking advantage of this, in 1610 the Poles attacked and conquered Moscow. However, the country was saved by a popular movement based in Nizhniy Novgorod and led by Kuzma Minnin, a merchant, and Duke Dmitri Pozharsky, an experienced fighting leader. After several bloody battles Moscow was liberated. In 1613 the Zemsky Sobor (State Council) assembled and elected as the new tsar Mikhail Romanov, who was the first of the dynasty that ruled Russia until 1917.

PETER THE GREAT AND THE 17TH CENTURY

In the course of the next 100 years, the feudal system continued to grow stronger in Russia and serfdom was established. The feudal lands were divided into those of the lords and those of the peasants. The peasant was allotted land; he worked his own plot as well as the landowner's, but he had to work the landowner's ground first, unpaid. He was, in effect, the landowner's slave. Under these terrible conditions peasant riots often broke out.

During this time, towns flourished and crafts developed. Trade also expanded successfully. Caviar, salt, and salted fish were shipped from Astrakhan to other towns; cloth and flax came from Novgorod, Yaroslavl, and Kostroma; leather came from Kazan; and furs from Siberia. Moscow and Nizhniy Novgorod were the largest trade centers. Russia continued to expand its territory into both Siberia and the Far East.

Ivan IV, known as "the Terrible." On his head is Monomakh's Cap, the oldest of the tsar's crowns. Legend has it that the crown was given to Vladimir Monomakh, prince of Kiev, by the Byzantine emperor Constantine Monomachus, in the 12th century. But the craftsmanship suggests it was of oriental origin and made in the 13th or 14th centuries.

Tsar Peter I was one of Russia's great reformers. His most far-reaching accomplishment was to draw Russia into the European sphere, which he achieved by transfering the capital to St. Petersburg, and by introducing European ideas and technology. Peter even went so far as to encourage European styles of dress.

PETER I In 1689, the 17-year-old Tsar Peter (1672–1725) inherited a huge country lagging considerably behind Europe, a result of the 200-year Tatar oppression that had greatly retarded its development. Russia did not have a developed industry, a modern army or navy, or any convenient sea harbors. The system of government was old, sluggish, and awkward. It was necessary to look for outlets to the sea as convenient ways for trade and cultural communication with Europe. The country also had to be able to defend itself against Europe's growing military might, and hence create Russia's own modern army and navy.

At that time, the Barents Sea was Russia's only naval outlet. But it was cold and ice-bound for six months of the year, as well as being too far from the center of Russia. The Baltic Sea coasts belonged to Sweden and the Black Sea coasts to Turkey. Russia gained an outlet to the Baltic Sea after extensive territorial gains from the Swedes in the Northern War.

In 1697 a great diplomatic mission left Moscow and went abroad to make alliances in Europe. The tsar himself traveled incognito, under the name of Peter Mikhailov, a sergeant of the infantry. Under this name he worked as a simple ship's carpenter at a shipyard in Holland. Later, in England, he studied shipbuilding theory and rose to the rank of engineer.

PETER'S REFORMS On his return from Europe, Peter introduced many reforms in Russia. He built metal works so that Russia could produce its own arms (by 1725, there were over 100 factories in Russia); he also started a textile industry. All trade was concentrated in St. Petersburg. A whole system of canals connecting the Neva River with the Volga was built in order to make it easier to transport goods from the south of the country to the north.

Peter divided the country into provinces headed by governors. Each governor was responsible for tax collection, the armed forces, and public

THE NORTHERN WAR (1700–21)

In the autumn of 1700, a war broke out against Sweden. It lasted for 21 years and was called the Northern War. The Russian army, badly armed, poorly fed, and badly trained, suffered many setbacks against the talented leadership of the Swedish King Charles XII (1682–1718). Peter decided to reform the Russian army. Some new regiments were formed and trained. Industrial enterprises were built to provide the army with the necessary hardware. There was not enough metal and Peter made a controversial decision: he ordered that church bells be melted into guns, and 300 new guns were cast. The reforms soon yielded results. The Russians won a great victory near Poltava (1709) against the Swedes. Charles was wounded and was nearly taken prisoner. The Nishtadt Treaty (1721) consolidated Russia's victories: Russia received land along the Baltic Sea coast and so became a European marine power. Following a drawing made by the tsar himself in 1703, the foundations of the Peter and Paul Fortress were laid on the boggy banks of the Neva River. Around this fortress the city-port of St. Petersburg developed, soon to become Russia's new capital.

order. The number of officials increased, and a complex bureaucratic machinery was formed to consolidate and maintain the ruling position of the gentry. The estates of the gentry were declared their hereditary property, strengthening the bonds of serfdom. This caused riots and occasional outbreaks of violence in the country.

Peter also introduced new schools; new textbooks on mathematics, navigation, physics, and chemistry were printed in Russia. He also opened an Academy of Science. All of Peter's reforms helped Russia overcome its industrial and cultural backwardness. As a result, Russia achieved a steep rise in the industrial, scientific, and technical spheres, and became a full-fledged European power.

CATHERINE II

The Russian Empire made great advances during the reign of Catherine II (1729–96), who has often been referred to as an "enlightened despot." The clever and educated empress introduced limited freedom of speech, and a liberal press appeared. However, behind the façade of the empress' liberal reasonings about the common welfare, a cruel form of serfdom flourished. A very serious peasant rebellion (1773–75) led by Emelyan Pugachev swept through Russia during her reign. It was the greatest

Peter I strongly discouraged the wearing of traditional beards by the gentry and aristocrats and had some of his more stubborn subjects' beards forcibly shaved off! Only the peasants and clergy were allowed to retain their beards, which Peter considered old-fashioned and not European enough.

popular revolt in Europe and shook the empire to its foundation. It involved the whole Volga region. Detachments of rebels conquered a series of towns—Kazan, Samara, Ufa, and Chelyabinsk—and burned down hundreds of landowners' estates. The army suppressed the uprising only with great difficulty.

FOREIGN AFFAIRS As a result of Russian alliances in Europe and of the divisions of Poland (1772, 1793, and 1795), Russia received a big part of the Ukrainian and Belorussian lands and a large part of Poland. Following two bloody wars with Turkey (1768–74 and 1787–91) the problem of gaining an outlet to the Black Sea was successfully solved, and the Crimean Peninsula and the Sea of Azov became Russian territory. Diplomatic relations with the United States were established: Russia proclaimed the Declaration of Armed Neutrality (1780), supporting the Americans' struggle against England.

THE PATRIOTIC WAR OF 1812

At the beginning of the 19th century, France invaded Russia, led by the Emperor Napoleon Bonaparte. Napoleon made no secret of the fact that he wanted to overrun Russia, to subdue and break the country, and distribute its territory among Turkey, Iran, and Poland.

One summer night in 1812, the French army of approximately 600,000 fighting men in three columns crossed the Neman River near Kovno (now Kaunas in Lithuania) without a declaration of war. Napoleon hoped to overwhelm the Russian army with one decisive blow, occupy Moscow, and dictate his terms. But instead, he found himself involved in a protracted war. The plan of encircling the Russian army failed, and the Russian army regrouped deep in its own territory. Under public pressure the popular

Catherine II reigned in Russia from 1762 to 1796. She gained the throne following a power struggle with her weak and unpopular husband, Tsar Peter III. Though German-born, Catherine loved her adopted country and, by carrying on the work begun by Peter the Great, led Russia into full participation in the political and cultural life of Europe.

Mikhail I. Kutuzov (1745–1813) became commander-in-chief of the Russian army. He decided to fight a decisive battle to undermine the French army's strength.

On September 7, 1812, on the fields near the village of Borodino, 70 miles (112.7 km) west of Moscow, half a million men fought each other in an exceptionally bloody battle. Neither side won decisively, but the Russians retreated and the French captured Moscow.

Kutuzov regrouped and strengthened his army, however, while Russian partisans (guerrillas) harassed French supply lines. The French army began to dwindle and retreated from Moscow. They suffered terribly from Russian attacks and the cruel winter. Of the 100,000 men in Napoleon's retreating army, only 9,000 managed to return to France.

THE 19TH CENTURY

The war of 1812 brought about a change in Russian national consciousness. The peasants, who had defended their country, returned to a life of slavish servitude under the landowners. The tsarist autocracy introduced *arakcheevschina* (after General Arakcheev, chief councillor to the tsar), a reactionary policy of merciless serfdom, military drill, and severe censorship. Military service, coupled with agricultural service, was required for life; peasant children began to receive military training at the age of 7 and at 18 were turned into soldiers. Understandably, these harsh policies caused much resentment.

THE DECEMBRISTS' REVOLT Consisting chiefly of patriotic young officers and intellectuals, these Romantic revolutionaries dreamed of

An 18th-century merchant's house. The merchant class grew steadily under the reforms of Tsar Peter I and Empress Catherine.

Field-Marshal Mikhail Kutuzov, commander-in-chief of the Russian army that defeated the French in 1812.

liberating the country from autocracy and bestowing a constitution upon Russia. They wanted Russia to become a constitutional monarchy. Because of the month in which they staged their protest, they became known as the Decembrists.

Following the death of Alexander I and the appointment of Nicholas I as the new Emperor, the conspiring officers led several garrisons to Senate Square in St. Petersburg on the morning of December 14, 1925; they called for freedom and change. The common people did not understand what they wanted and did not support them. On the tsar's orders, they were fired upon and, by nightfall, they retreated.

Altogether 579 people were brought to trial and more than 100 were sentenced to penal servitude and exile in Siberia. Five leaders—P. Pestel, K. Ryleev, S. Muraviev-Apostol, M. Bestuzhev-Ryumin, and P. Kakhovsky—were hanged. But these young conspirators' actions would continue to inspire future generations of revolutionaries and reformers.

After the suppression of the Decembrists' revolt, the reactionary regime of Nicholas I was established and lasted for over 30 years. He was a rough, cruel man who ruled with the precision and intolerance of a military dictator. Even the slightest criticism of the government was punished. Educational establishments were under vigilant supervision, and strict censorship was introduced in literature. Peasant disturbances were mercilessly suppressed. After many years of war, the northern

Caucasus region became Russian—with the Chechens, Dagestanis, and other Caucasian peoples losing their independence.

THE CRIMEAN WAR The direct clash of Russian and Turkish interests in their struggle for influence in the Balkan region led to the Crimean War (1853–56). Russian successes in the opening stages of the war led to England and France joining the war against Russia. Most of the fighting occurred in the Crimea, where a force of over 60,000 English, French, and Turkish troops laid siege to the Russian naval base of Sevastopol. For more than 11 months the garrison and the inhabitants repelled enemy attacks, and the allies managed to capture it only at great cost to themselves. After finally defeating Russia, the allies gained a favorable peace settlement, temporarily putting an end to Russia's ambitions in the Balkans.

The revolt on the Senate Square in St. Petersburg, December, 1825, a water-color painted in 1830 by K. Coelman, depicting the Decembrists' Revolt.

ABOLITION OF SERFDOM Losing the war increased opposition to the tsar among the progressive gentry. Peasant disturbances also increased. Under these conditions, Tsar Alexander II (1818–81), the son of Nicholas I, who had died in 1855, said: "It is better to abolish serfdom from above than to wait for a time when it will begin to abolish itself from below."

Serfdom was abolished on February 19, 1861. The peasants gained their personal freedom—a landowner no longer had the right to buy or sell them. A peasant could get married without the permission of the landowner, could conclude contracts and bargains on his own, and could engage in his choice of handicrafts and commerce. The peasants became free citizens with full rights. However, some things did not change; peasants continued to pay a poll tax, and were subject to corporal punishment and military service. In addition, a peasant could leave his village only after paying off all his debts to the landowner, and although the peasants were freed together with the land, the best lands remained in the hands of the landowners.

Reforms were also made at the local government level, with the creation of the *zemstvos* (ZYEMST-vo)—a committee responsible for the development of the economy and infrastructure in their region. The law was made more accessible to the majority of people, and schools were opened for the common people.

In the latter half of the 19th century, Russia gradually transformed from a feudal agrarian society to an emerging capitalist industrial power. Food processing, textiles, and machine-producing industries began to flourish. Railroad construction expanded on a massive scale from 1860 to 1890. By the end of the century, the Trans-Siberian railroad connecting western Russia with the Far East had been completed.

However, peasant rebellions continued because of the limited reforms. Secret revolutionary societies, composed of the educated, made their appearance, and it was one of these—Narodnaya Volya (People's Freedom)—that in March 1881 assassinated Tsar Alexander II. Alexander III (1845–94), the new tsar, established a regime of brutal

Troika (1866), a painting by Vasily Perov. Life for the vast majority of Russians was one of back-breaking drudgery in the 19th century. The title is intended ironically, since a troika is usually a vehicle drawn by three horses, not children.

regression. The leaders of Narodnaya Volya were put to death. But workers' disturbances continued, and the first workers' unions were established. In the 1890s, Vladimir Ilyich Lenin began his revolutionary activities in Russia, and in 1903 founded the Communist Party, the party that later ruled Russia for more than 70 years.

In 1894 a new tsar, Nicholas II (1868–1917), came to the throne.

WORLD WAR I

In the summer of 1914, World War I broke out. Russia, along with Britain and France, was drawn into a vast and protracted war against Germany, Austria-Hungary, and Italy. By 1917 Russia's strength was on the brink of exhaustion. Against a background of industrial disintegration, an aggravated food crisis developed and a feeling of discontent with the government and the unsuccessful war gripped the population. The great losses sustained at the front, economic chaos, and the growing revolutionary crisis at home undermined the morale of the Russian troops. In the tsarist court, Grigory Rasputin (1872–1916), a self-styled "saint," exerted unlimited influence on the tsarina, who believed he could heal her son of hemophilia. Rasputin was murdered by aristocratic army officers in 1916.

Nicholas II, the last tsar of Russia, with his wife Alexandra, both in ceremonial garb.

THE REVOLUTIONS OF 1917

The year 1917 began with an unprecedented wave of strikes. There were endless demonstrations on Nevsky Prospekt, St. Petersburg's main

THE 1905 REVOLUTION

In Russia, the 20th century began with the unsuccessful war against Japan (1904–105) for domination in Manchuria, northern China. The Japanese dealt Russia a number of defeats on land and at sea that demonstrated the backwardness of the Russian army, as well as the appalling corruption in the military and state systems.

It was dissatisfaction with this war that ignited the events of January 9, 1905. On that day, soldiers fired upon a peaceful demonstration of workers who were marching to the Winter Palace in St. Petersburg with a petition outlining the people's needs. More than 1,000 workers were killed and 5,000 wounded. This brutal action provoked a storm of public indignation. On the same evening, the city was covered with a network of barricades erected by the incensed population. Workers disarmed policemen and took their weapons. General strikes occurred in many cities and the peasants revolted in the countryside. A revolt even broke out on board the battleship *Potemkin* in the Black Sea. The peak of the revolution came in December—involving armed revolts in Kharkov, Rostov-on-Don, Sormovo, and Krasnovarsk. The largest uprising was in Moscow.

For almost two weeks, government forces were unable to suppress the uprising. The government managed to destroy resistance only after using heavy artillery. Many reprisals followed—unions were banned, newspapers and magazines were liquidated, and many revolutionaries and workers were executed.

thoroughfare, and many clashes with the police. Troops began to support the insurgents, and the city was soon in the hands of the workers and soldiers. The Soviet (Council) of Workers' and Soldiers' Deputies of Petrograd (the new name given to St. Petersburg) was set up.

The Duma (state council) established a provisional committee that included representatives of all political parties. On March 15, Nicholas II abdicated. Nicholas and his family were later murdered by Bolshevik revolutionaries in 1918 in Yekaterinburg in the Urals.

Officially, the country was ruled by the provisional government headed by Prince George Lvov (1861–1925), a famous *zemstvo* leader. But actually the Petrograd Soviet and other soviets around the country held much of the power.

On June 3, 1917, the first All-Russian Congress of Soviets of Workers' and Soldiers' Deputies opened in Petrograd, at which the RSDWP (the abbreviation for the Communist Party) declared its readiness to take power. A month later, on July 3, after armed workers and soldiers tried to seize power, the provisional government went on the offensive. People were arrested and workers' demonstrations were fired upon. The provisional government quickly lost the confidence of the people, since it was unable to end food shortages or the unpopular war with Germany.

On November 7, the revolutionary Red Guard workers, soldiers, and sailors stormed the Winter Palace in St. Petersburg and arrested the members of the provisional government. There were several reasons for their easy victory. The Communist Party was one of the biggest in the country. It numbered more than 200,000 members at that time, was well-organized and disciplined, and was represented everywhere—even in the army and navy. For many years, the party had spread its ideas among all sections of the population, and advanced simple slogans that were comprehensible to the masses, such as "Land—To Those Who Till It," and "He Who Does Not Work Shall Not Eat."

Above: **Alexander Kerensky, a leader of the provisional government established by the Duma in 1917 after Tsar Nicholas' abdication.**

Opposite: **Vladimir Ilyich Lenin, the founder of the Communist Party in Russia, speaks to a crowd in 1917.**

During the first months after the revolution, the new power nationalized land, banks, transportation, and large-scale industry, and established a state monopoly on foreign trade. By signing the disadvantageous and "revolting" (as Lenin called it) Brest Treaty, Russia ended its war with Germany, and ceded the Baltic regions, part of Ukraine, and Belarus to Germany.

CIVIL WAR There followed a terrible and bloody civil war (1918–22), during which the Communists (Reds) and monarchists (Whites) fought for control of Russia. The situation was further complicated by the intervention of foreign powers—Britain, France, Germany, Japan, and the United States—who wanted to restore the old order and supported the Whites. But it was the Reds who were ultimately victorious. Their promise to redistribute the land to the peasants generated a lot of grassroots support. Leon Trotsky (1879–1940), commander-in-chief, restored discipline and fighting efficiency to the army via draconian methods. The Red army was able to defeat the White generals and their supporters and allies. In 1922 the last foreign troops left Russia and the Communists—under the leadership of Lenin and Trotsky—were able to celebrate their victory.

FORMATION OF THE USSR

After the November 1917 Revolution and subsequent civil war, the former empire broke into several independent socialist republics—including Russia, Ukraine, and Belorussia (now called Belarus). After the civil war, the necessity for economic and political cooperation became evident. In 1922, representatives of four republics—Russia, Ukraine, Belorussia , and Transcaucasia (now Georgia, Armenia, and Azerbaijan)—signed a declaration forming the Union of Soviet Socialist Republics (USSR). During the 1930s, Kazakhstan, Uzbekistan, Turkmenistan, Kyrgyzstan, and Tajikistan joined the USSR; the Baltic states (Estonia, Latvia, and Lithuania) were annexed by the USSR in 1940 at the beginning of World War II.

In January 1924, Lenin, the founder of the Soviet state and the Communist Party, died. A bitter power struggle followed his death, with Joseph Stalin (1879–1953) eventually winning the leadership as general secretary of

Leon Trotsky was one of the original leaders of the 1917 Revolution. He was a great military tactician and rousing public speaker, considered by many people to be a greater and more imaginative social and political theorist than Lenin. Trotsky was exiled from Russia in 1928, having failed in a power struggle with the more ruthless Joseph Stalin. Perceived as an ideological threat by the paranoid Stalinist regime, he was assassinated by Stalinist agents while exiled in Mexico in 1940.

the Communist Party. He was to impose his ruthless dictatorship for the next 30 years.

Stalin's reign of terror in Russia reached its height in 1937. Books and films were heavily censored, and only those praising Stalin and the Communist Party were allowed. Any opposition to the regime was regarded as a state crime, punishment being death or imprisonment in one of the many labor camps established in the Soviet Union. Purge followed purge, ostensibly in search of counter-revolutionaries and spies—but in fact the fear and suspicion generated was Stalin's way of increasing his hold on power.

In order to implement Lenin's blueprint for modernizing Russia in the 1920s and 1930s, modern branches of industry were created and small farms were forcibly collectivized. In the course of collectivization, the famine of 1931 in Ukraine claimed about 10 million lives. All land became state-owned. With no individual responsibility, agricultural output kept declining, and the largest country in the world found it could not feed itself and had to buy its grain abroad.

A huge poster with the faces of the three ideologists upon which Soviet Communism was founded: Karl Marx, Friedrich Engels, and Vladimir Ilyich Lenin. One of Marx's more famous pronouncements was "From each according to his means, to each according to his needs." He envisioned an egalitarian society where everybody was equally provided for, and where the wealthy and strong would support the disadvantaged.

COMMUNISM

Communism is a political and economic doctrine based on the holding of all property in common, actual ownership being ascribed to the community as a whole or to the state. Modern Communism is considered to have been founded by Karl Marx (1818–83) and Friedrich Engels (1820–95), with the publication of the *Communist Manifesto* in 1848, and later expounded in more detail in Marx's monumental *Das Capital* (1866–94).

Big improvements were made in education and healthcare. From 1920 to 1940, almost 50 million men and women became literate. In 1930 universal primary education was introduced. Russia was also the first country in the world to introduce free health care for all its people.

WORLD WAR II

Russia feared invasion when Hitler rose to power in Germany in 1933. One of his many aims was to destroy Communism. Stalin had tried to avoid confrontation with Germany by signing a secret nonaggression pact with Hitler in 1939. On June 22, 1941, Nazi Germany attacked the USSR. Six

Right: **Russian troops officially celebrate victory over the Germans at the end of World War II with a parade in Red Square, June 24, 1945.**

Opposite: **Marshal Georgy Zhukov (1896–1974), the commander who launched the successful counter-offensive against the Germans in 1942–43. Zhukov was a chief member of Stalin's supreme headquarters and was instrumental in the planning and execution of almost every major engagement in World War II.**

months later, German troops occupied half of the western part of the Soviet Union. They laid siege to Leningrad and were stopped just short of the gates of Moscow, but managed to reach the Volga in the south.

Financial and military aid was provided to Russia by Britain and the United States. A breakthrough was achieved early in 1943 following the five-month Battle of Stalingrad. The Germans were eventually driven from Russian lands in 1944, and Soviet troops entered Berlin on May 1, 1945. It is estimated that more than 20 million Russian soldiers and civilians died in World War II.

PERIOD OF RECONSTRUCTION

In the postwar period, Stalin, suspicious of his wartime Western allies, consolidated wartime gains in Eastern Europe and ensured Communist dominance there. An "iron curtain" of barbed wire and observation towers was built to segregate Eastern Europe from the West. A nuclear arms race with the United States ensued, consuming enormous resources.

After Stalin died in 1953, restrictions were loosened under the new general secretary, Nikita Khrushchev (1894–1971). Thousands of people who had been jailed under Stalin were set free and the country made some outstanding achievements—launching the first artificial satellite and then the first man in space, Yuri Gagarin. Housing was improved and thousands of families were given apartments. However, Khrushchev's experiments in agriculture led to a further weakening of the economy. In 1964, as a result of internal

Above: **Yuri Gagarin (1934–68), Russian cosmonaut who, in 1961, became the first man to travel into space.**

Opposite: **Mikhail Gorbachev became leader of the Communist Party in 1985, and quickly ushered in the reforms of *glasnost* (openness) and *perestroika* (restructuring). He was president of the USSR from 1990 to 1991, but with the break-up of the USSR into independent republics, each republic has its own leadership.**

politics, Khrushchev was removed from power. A period of stagnation followed.

PARTY COLLAPSE

This period was associated with the new general secretary, Leonid Brezhnev (1906–82). It was a period of superficial prosperity, but underlying decay. As time passed, the USSR found itself ruled by a group of old men totally out of touch with the outside world. The disintegration of society was accelerated by the war in Afghanistan.

In 1985 the new general secretary, Mikhail S. Gorbachev (b. 1931), tried to save the Party and the country with widespread reforms. He brought an end to the war in Afghanistan; set many political prisoners free, among them the famous nuclear scientist and human rights advocate Andrei Sakharov; and tried to reform the economy and democratize the government. Yet he was hated by the old guard, Communists who were afraid of losing their power. In August 1991, they attempted to remove Gorbachev and reinstate the old Communist system. The coup was defeated by reform-minded Russians led by Boris Yeltsin (b. 1931), who was later elected as the country's new leader.

The unsuccessful coup of 1991 and the emergence of Boris Yeltsin as a powerful political figure marked a turn in events in Russia's political history. The USSR, a unified and powerful state for so long, disintegrated in December 1991, splitting up into 15 independent countries: the Russian Federation, Lithuania, Latvia, Estonia, Belarus, Ukraine, Moldova, Kazakhstan, Turkmenistan, Uzbekistan, Kyrgyzstan, Tajikistan, Georgia, Azerbaijan, and Armenia. Today, 12 republics cooperate as the

Commonwealth of Independent States (CIS). The Baltic republics—Latvia, Lithuania, and Estonia—chose not to join the CIS and remain totally independent of Russia.

Yeltsin's immediate concern was to lift Russia's ailing economy out of the doldrums by moving it toward private enterprise and free trade. Yeltsin was reelected in July 1996 but soon suffered a heart attack. This affected his health but he remained in office until 1999. On December 31, he stepped down and named Vladimir Putin (b. 1952) as his successor.

CONFLICT IN CHECHNYA

Conflict arose in the republic of Chechnya when Russian troops were sent to subdue the Chechen independence movement, led by Dzhokhar Dudayev, on December 31, 1994. This led to a protracted conflict between the Chechen rebels and Russian troops, and the ongoing war was a major issue during the 1996 presidential elections. Aleksandr I. Lebed (1950–2002) fared well in the first round of voting and was promoted to the position of Security Adviser by President Yeltsin in an effort to gain the votes of Lebed's supporters.

Lebed was able to negotiate a ceasefire in September 1996, but it is estimated that 80,000 lives were lost in nearly two years of fighting. Lebed was removed from his position in Yeltsin's government in October 1996 and died in a helicopter crash in 2002.

Several years after the ceasefire, the war reignited and continued into the 21st century.

GOVERNMENT

PRIOR TO 1991 the USSR consisted of 15 republics controlled by a centralized federal government and parliament. Russia was the largest republic. Each republic had a small-scale governmental structure, ruled by a local representative body called a soviet. Soviets were the primary elected political organizations and were composed of peasants, workers, and soldiers known as Soviets of People's Deputies.

The Congress of People's Deputies was the highest body of state authority. This Congress elected a standing legislature called the Supreme Soviet. It consisted of two chambers: the Council of the Union and the Council of Nationalities. The Supreme Soviet appointed the Council of Ministers, which was the executive body of the government.

In the republics the highest authority was the Congress of People's Deputies of that republic. The republic's Supreme Soviet was a body accountable to the Congress. The Congress formed the Council of Ministers, who constituted the republic's executive branch. This complicated, multi-tier, governmental structure was no more than a façade. The Communist Party of the Soviet Union (CPSU) was the only party in the USSR, all other parties having been destroyed or outlawed after the 1917 Revolution and ensuing civil war. From the Supreme Soviet down, all positions of authority were held by CPSU members.

All ministers and trade-union leaders were nominated by the executive body of the CPSU's central committee, the Politburo. The general secretary of the Party was the chairman of the Politburo and generally viewed as the top ruler of the USSR.

Following in this tradition, the general secretary of the CPSU, Mikhail Gorbachev, became the country's first president when the presidency was instituted in the USSR in 1990. This tradition was finally broken in Russia

Any citizen over age 18 could be elected as a people's deputy, and anyone over age 21 could be a federal people's deputy. The deputies performed their duties as volunteers and would be granted a leave of absence from their permanent jobs to attend a congress or session.

Opposite: **The view of the Kremlin from the other side of the river. The Kremlin is the seat of government of the Russian Federation.**

when Boris Yeltsin, a high-ranking official who had withdrawn from the Communist Party, was elected as the Russian Federation's first president in 1991. During his tenure there was constant conflict between him and members of the Supreme Soviet. In 1993 Yeltsin dissolved the parliament in order to hold new democratic elections, but hardline members barricaded themselves in the parliament building and refused to accept the president's decree. It ended in bloodshed when troops stormed the building.

Since the break-up of the USSR, the Russian Federation has embarked on a program of reform to bring about greater freedom and democracy. Several signs of this are democratic elections, multiple political parties, and government restructuring.

On December 12, 1993, Russia held its first democratic, multi-party elections. No party won a decisive victory in the 450-seat parliament and approximately eight parties emerged, each gaining more than 5 percent of the votes, with many other candidates gaining individual seats. The result meant that the three main political groups—the pro-Yeltsin reformist Russia's Choice (30 percent), the Communists (12 percent), and the nationalist Liberal Democratic Party (23 percent), and the independent candidates had to cooperate for any coherent government policy to emerge.

Shortly after the elections a new constitution was adopted and a new government was established. The constitution was written in a way that protects the civil rights of all Russian citizens.

Voters register at a polling station in Kiev, Ukraine. Since 1991, Ukraine has been politically independent from the old USSR, and now holds separate elections. The former countries of the USSR now retain a loose unity under the banner of the Commonwealth of Independent States (CIS), formed in December 1991.

CURRENT GOVERNMENT STRUCTURE

The Russian president is elected by the citizens to act as head of state for a four-year term. The president appoints the premier to serve as head of government and ranking official of the Council of Ministers cabinet, which oversees government operations.

The Federal Assembly, or parliament, is made up of a 450-member lower house, or State Duma, and a 178-member upper house, or Federation Council, that makes Russian laws. Members are elected for four-year terms and include regional governors and local legislature leaders. All legislation must be approved by the president and Federation Council before becoming law.

Local governments are divided into 49 *oblasts* (territories named after large cities), 21 self-governing republics that represent each dominant ethnic group, 10 autonomous *okrugs* or districts, six *krays* (smaller territories that represent the ethnic minorities), one autonomous *oblast*, and two cities, Moscow and St. Petersburg, which have federal status.

The highest judicial body in Russia is the Constitutional Court, which was established in 1991 and governs all Russian laws. There is also a Supreme Court and a Superior Court of Arbitration. On the recommendation of the president, judges for the various courts are appointed by the Federation Council to serve a life term. The chief Russian legal officer is the prosecutor-general.

LAW ENFORCEMENT

Under Soviet rule the Committee on State Security (KGB) influenced the way in which the law was enforced. As a result, many human-rights violations occurred. Today the KGB has been replaced with two national

Since 1993, Russia has held three democratic presidential elections. In 1996 Boris Yeltsin was reelected to a second term. Upon his resignation, Vladimir Putin was named as acting president. In 2000 Putin was elected president by popular vote. He was reelected in 2004 with a majority vote of more than 70 percent. During his years in office, Putin has sought to end corruption and move Russia toward a full-market economy.

Born in Yekaterinburg, Boris Yeltsin worked in the construction industry while working his way up through the party ranks at both the regional and national levels. He was a member of the Supreme Soviet from 1989 to 1991. He became the first president of the Russian Federation in 1991.

security agencies. The Federal Security Service (previously known as the Federal Counterintelligence Service) enforces laws that affect internal security, and the Foreign Intelligence Service enforces laws that affect external security.

MAJOR POLITICAL PARTIES

The Communist Party was the only government party until 1991 when other political parties were formed. The first of these was the Democratic Russia movement which supported Yeltsin in his move to be elected president in 1991, as well as in his 1996 reelection.

Since 1991 a number of other political parties have emerged. During the latest State Duma elections in December 2003, the United Russia party, formed in 2001, won a landslide victory with 37.6 percent of the total vote. The Communist Party of the Russian Federation (KPRF) was formed in 1993 and had the most number of seats during the 1995 and 1999 elections. However, the party only managed to garner about 12.6 percent of the total vote in 2003. Founded in 1990, the Liberal Democratic Party of Russia (LDPR) maintains conservative Communist beliefs. The LDPR has sought an end to economic reforms and promotes taking back control of the former Soviet republics. In 2003, the party attained 11.5 percent of the votes.

The People's Patriotic Union, better known as the Motherland bloc, was formed in 1993 just before the elections of that year in order for the nationalist and left-wing supporters to be heard. In 2003 the party received 9 percent of the votes.

Formed in 1993, a group called Yabloko, which means apple in Russian, aimed to make life normal for the Russian people. Support for the party was strong in previous elections, but in 2003 Yabloko won only 4.3 percent of the vote. Failing to gain at least 5 percent of the total vote, Yabloko is not represented as a party in the State Duma.

FOREIGN RELATIONS

Since the breakup of the USSR, Russia's political relationship with its 14 former republics has not always been positive. There have been many concerns regarding defense weapons, border security, and ethnic conflict. One of these concerns is the ongoing war with Chechnya that continues until today. However, whenever possible, agreements have been made and treaties signed in order to ensure that relations continue to evolve in a positive direction.

In 1994 Russia signed a partnership and cooperation agreement with the European Union (EU). In 2003 Putin became the first Russian leader to visit the United Kingdom since 1874.

The charismatic Vladimir Putin was reelected to a second and final term as president in March 2004.

The United States and Russia have maintained good relations despite a few difficult periods, such as Putin's refusal to support U.S. military operations in Iraq. In 1997 Russia and the North Atlantic Treaty Organization (NATO) signed the NATO-Russia Founding Act. This treaty, however, has been superceded by the NATO-Russia Council signed in 2002, which gives Russia a voice in policies concerning peacekeeping and weapons management.

ECONOMY

AFTER THE 1917 REVOLUTION an attempt was made by the Communists to create an economy based on socialist principles. They believed the capitalist system led to chaotic economic development, cruel exploitation of workers, unemployment, and overproduction crises. Their socialist economy would rest on two basic principles formulated by Karl Marx: public ownership of the means of production (factories, mines, industry, and agriculture) and a centrally planned economy. One of the first decisions made by the Communists was to nationalize industrial plants and factories and all their equipment, as well as banks and capital.

Later, in 1929–30, under the process of collectivization, the land became state-owned (state farms) and cooperatively owned (collective farms). There was no longer any private land ownership. Cattle also belonged to the state. The state became the monopolist in the economy. The Communists believed that since the means of production belonged to the state (and hence, collectively, to the people, because a socialist state is a state belonging to the people), the state should control everything, including planning, financing, and salaries. Under this system, people were supposed to be content and to work peacefully for the benefit of society.

Over the long term, this style of economy failed. Under this system, there was no reason for the common man, or anyone who was not a fanatical supporter of the socialist ideal, to work hard or to improve or create anything. Centralized planning also had a ruinous effect; workers and peasants merely had to fulfil the orders passed from above regardless of their practicality. This sometimes resulted in goods being produced that nobody needed and seed being sown into barren or frozen soil. Personal initiative was neither encouraged nor expected.

During the 1980s major funds were spent on producing weapons for the Cold War with the United States. Capital investments needed the

Abolishing private ownership of businesses and land killed people's desire to succeed or to create and increase their own assets. The driving force of personal gain was absent from all work activity. The socialist philosophy assumed that tireless and selfless labor for the benefit of society which would earn the worker a subsistence wage and succeed in bringing good life for all.

Opposite: **A sign of the changing times. These ladies selling dried goods at a local market now work for themselves.**

economy to grow and to maintain a decent standard of living were practically nonexistent and the Soviet economy stalled.

POST SOVIET ECONOMY

Under Soviet rule, the country lived on "petrodollars" by selling oil and gas at low prices. However, that did not last long. Rivalry in the arms race with the United States devoured tremendous wealth. Moreover, much money and energy were spent on supporting "friendly" Communist regimes in Asia, Africa, the Caribbean, and Central and South America.

Russia's economic contacts with former republics were weak. The country lacked sufficient hard currency to purchase raw goods and semi-finished materials needed for manufacturing. Inflation and high-priced goods resulted in the decline of an individual's purchasing capacity.

Oil production, which was a major source of profit, sagged and metal production was strangled by the lack of raw materials. The engineering industry continued to stagnate because of a drop in demand brought about by high prices. This was also the case in the chemical, oil, forestry, manufacturing, and food industries.

Another hurdle citizens had to overcome was the change in the way goods were produced. A society where practically everything was government-planned instantly became a society where people were forced to plan, provide, and produce for themselves. No one was prepared for such rapid change, and something had to be done quickly if the economy was to survive.

ECONOMIC REFORM BEGINS

Boris Yeltsin wanted radical economic reforms that would help create a fluid democratic economy. In 1992 he ended price controls on most purchased goods, lifted restrictions on private trade, and began to transfer state-owned enterprises into private ownership.

The Russian people immediately felt the effects of these drastic changes. Prices on most goods increased drastically, while industrial production and national income plummeted. By 1993 more than one third of Russian citizens were classified as living below the poverty line. Many wealthy citizens moved abroad.

Despite many challenges, by the mid-1990s more than a million new private businesses had been established, employing more than two-thirds of the labor force. Most money-making opportunities from business ownership or employment were available only in large cities such as Moscow and St. Petersburg.

In 1998 the Russian government defaulted on its foreign loans, and shortly thereafter an economic crisis occurred. The value of the ruble plummeted, and there was widespread economic hardship. This magnified the existing problems, and many of Russia's intellectual citizens emigrated to other countries, seeking better standards of living.

By 2001 the economy began to show healthy signs of steady recovery from the inflation of the 1990s. Three-fourths of formerly state-owned enterprises were now privately owned, and a middle-class population was growing. This led to a boom in consumer purchases of goods and services that had previously only been available to the wealthy.

Russian women working on a collective farm near Novgorod.

THE 21ST CENTURY

AGRICULTURE Prior to the Soviet regime's collapse there were about 15,000 state-controlled farms, which were run like factories using an inadequate production process. Farmland was divided into collectives of about 30,000 acres each and further divided into plots. A family was assigned to work each plot on the collective, and the government purchased the produce at a set price.

Even with the government's attempt to privatize farms, this changed very little. By 1993 about 90 percent of farmland was still controlled by former state farms or collectives, which had been restructured as cooperatives or joint stock companies. The main problem was that people who worked the land for a living could not afford to buy it. Also, agricultural output and grain production in Russia had traditionally been low due to the short growing season, inconsistent climate, and poor, quality soil.

In 2002 a new law granted the right for citizens to own, buy, sell, and transfer private agricultural land. However, private farm ownership has only increased marginally, by about 6 percent.

A combine harvester at work near Kaliningrad. Though a part of the Russian Federation, Kaliningrad is land-locked by Poland to the south and Lithuania to the east.

MILITARY DEFENSE Russia's military defense industry includes weapons manufacturing and aircraft building. Under the Soviet government they had a major place in the world market and were leaders in supplying countries worldwide. While weapons are still produced they are no longer a significant part of Russia's economy.

One example is the world's most widely used assault rifle, the AK 47 (Kalashnikov). This weapon was invented in Russia in 1947 and remains the basic weapon of the Russian army and other Communist countries. It is still manufactured in Russia but the market has declined. Many versions are produced outside Russia, in countries such as the United States, Bulgaria, China, Germany, Hungary, North Korea, Poland, and Romania.

AEROSPACE INDUSTRY   Aircraft production in the Russian Federation declined after 1991 but it did not die. This may be attributed to Russian products such as the IL-86 broad-fuselage liner, manufactured at the Voronezh aviation plant. This is the only series-produced liner that has never had an accident. On the basis of the successful design of the IL-86, the subsonic passenger jet IL-96-300 was built. Russia's civilian aircraft production has dropped to five or fewer airplanes annually. Today Aeroflot relies on Boeing planes for flights to the United States because of their higher fuel efficiency.

SPACE INDUSTRY   Russia remains a world leader in rocket-engine production and extended space travel. However, the space program is not as active as it once was due to budget cuts. In 2000 President Putin signed a Federal Space Program bill that supports funding to replace some of the more than 100 space satellites in orbit with new communications technology.

The United States, Japan, France, and China are also providing assistance for Russia's space program.

An atomic machine-building plant in the Ural Mountains.

NATURAL RESOURCES Russia possesses incalculable natural resources including oil, coal, gas, metal ores, precious stones, gold, silver, platinum, vast forests, and hydroelectric power.

Most mining and refining of natural resources takes place in the Ural Mountains and along the Volga River. While high quantities of these resources are available, there is much more in the eastern part of the

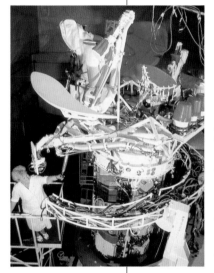

The aerial section of an orbital space communications unit is assembled at the Polyot Industrial Association in Omsk. Russia has built a highly successful space industry.

country that remains untapped. This is mainly due to the harsh weather, and rugged, sometimes uninhabited, land.

The country's largest source of economic income is from gas, oil, metals, and timber, which account for more than 80 percent of its exports.

INDUSTRIAL MANUFACTURING Russia's manufacturing industry is currently in need of modernization in order to become more efficient and provide a wider range of economic support. Production machinery is outdated and many buildings housing the equipment are old and dilapidated.

The manufacturing industry includes chemicals, farming equipment, electric power generators, durable goods, textiles, foodstuff, and handicrafts. These goods are mostly produced in large cities like St. Petersburg and Moscow. People who seek more job opportunities and higher income must often relocate to these cities from rural areas of the country.

SERVICE INDUSTRY Since Russia opened its borders to outsiders, several new service industries have developed that contribute to the economy. It is estimated that in 2002 about 65 percent of the labor force was engaged in the service industry.

The tourism industry in Russia is booming. Travel agencies in St. Petersburg and Moscow offer organized tours, from hiking and rafting adventures to train excursions and historical city tours.

Russians are also wired for communication. There are about 8,000 private broadcast companies, including radio and television, more than 560,000 Internet service providers, and the industry shows no sign of

slowing down. People in Russia have access to the latest technological advances—such as cell phones and video games—just like people in other developed countries.

MANPOWER Despite the population decrease, Russia has enough labor power to drive its economy. In 2003 it was estimated that the labor force was 72 million. Unemployment is only 8.5 percent, but underemployment is still a big problem.

Russia has faced many challenges and setbacks, but the country's economy shows signs of healthy improvement. The gross domestic product (GDP) in 2003 was 7.3 percent, and high oil prices have allowed Russia to increase its foreign reserves. The country has kept a high trade surplus and met foreign debt payments, drastically reducing the amounts from 90 to 28 percent since 1998. Inflation was estimated to be 13.7 percent in 2003, and foreign investments had doubled from the previous year.

Fishermen haul in their nets on the Volga River near Astrakhan. Russia's future economic success will depend greatly on the efforts of its vast labor force.

ENVIRONMENT

RUSSIA'S CURRENT ENVIRONMENTAL CHALLENGES have their roots in its heavy industrial production while under Communist rule. During the Soviet years, great emphasis was placed on industry and weapon development with no regard for environmental care. Many years of improper waste disposal have resulted in heavy pollution of the land, air, and water.

MINING

Russia is one of the richest sources of natural minerals in the world. The minerals required in industrial production are in high demand both in Russia and abroad. Mining and exporting gold, platinum, copper, iron, nickel, coal, and precious stones are lucrative economic activities for Russia. Unfortunately, this desperately needed source of income also takes a heavy environmental toll on the land.

Mining has been profitable for the country, but the result has been nearly catastrophic. As far back as the 18th century, minerals have been extracted from the Ural Mountains. Mining may take years to completely deplete an area of its minerals, but once the resources are gone, they cannot be replenished. Also, heavy extraction of the earth's natural resources destabilizes the land, and alternative forms of use are difficult to identify.

OIL DRILLING

Oil spills cause major environmental problems because they are difficult to clean up. At this time no method has been developed that does a completely efficient job. Once a body of water is contaminated with oil, it can destroy aquatic life and make the water uninhabitable for many years.

Above: **A metal processing factory.**

Opposite: **Picking cabbages from a garden built on land that has since recovered from the Chernobyl nuclear accident of 1986.**

In 2003 Russia was the second largest supplier of crude oil in the world after Saudi Arabia. The Russian government forecast total oil production in 2004 at nine and a half million barrels per day, most of it to be exported to Europe. Russia holds an estimated 60 billion barrels of oil in reserve.

The oil and natural gas industries are vital to the Russian economy, but exploration, production, and spills have taken a toll on the land. Although oil production has decreased since Soviet days, when daily production targets were set, most Russian oil refineries are old and inefficiently designed. As a result, they do not adhere to modern environmental requirements for oil production.

AIR POLLUTION

An environmental report issued in 2002 by the Russian government indicated that air pollution in most major cities exceeds safe levels, and safe drinking water is also at risk. These contribute to health problems such as chronic respiratory disorders, heart disease, and high cancer rates. More than 30 percent of Russian children

Working in the oil field.

are born with pollution-linked diseases or physical defects. Emissions from road traffic, heavy industry, and coal-fired power plants contribute to unhealthy levels of toxins in the air.

Over the past decade many Russian citizens have moved from small towns to large cities such as Moscow and St. Petersburg to find work. Since more vehicles are required for inner-city transportation, pollution in large cities is greater than in small towns.

Other major contributors to air pollution are Russia's iron and steel manufacturing plants, some of which have been in operation for more than 50 years. Several cities were established with the sole purpose of supporting iron and steel production. The cities of Perm, Chelyabinsk, and Magnitogorsk are examples, and they continue to be the locations for major industrial manufacturers today.

The city of Perm dates back to 1723, when it was established for copper smelting. The city provided easy access to the Volga River and was part of an important transportation route. Today it remains a heavily industrialized city with approximately 80 factories that represent the aircraft, electrical, chemical, oil, timber, and engineering industries.

In 1929 the province (city) of Chelyabinsk was established on the bank of the Ural River for the purpose of mining the area's iron ore. In the mid-1970s the plants here produced 15 million tons of ore per year. That eventually led to the depletion of the iron ore deposits.

Magnitogorsk, built on the site of iron ore deposits, is the largest steel milling town in the world. Developed in 1929–31 under the first Five-Year Plan, it became a symbol of Soviet industrial growth. In 1996 it produced 7.5 million tons of steel. However, its production has been declining sharply recently, and air pollution is a serious problem.

Many rivers in Russia are polluted by the run-off from factories, and households.

WATER POLLUTION

Most freshwater sources in Russia are polluted. The Russian Environment Ministry estimates freshwater resource damage will cost an estimated $2.3 billion to correct. Most of the water is contaminated from sewage and manufacturing runoff. Some freshwater sources are the Kola and Selenga rivers, and Lake Baikal.

The Kola River is located in the Kola Peninsula of the Arctic region that borders the Barents and the White Sea. The Kola Peninsula covers 40,000 square miles (100,000 square km) and is the world's largest supplier of phosphorus. The contaminants released there affect the freshwater and marine ecosystems. In addition, the Kola River is one of several rivers that release pollutants into the Arctic Ocean.

The Selenga River is located in east-central Russia and is the main source of water for Lake Baikal. Domestic waste from large cities and industrial waste from chemical plants and pulp and paper mills contribute to its pollution.

Lake Baikal is located in southern Siberia. It is a clear blue, banana-shaped body of freshwater surrounded by a vast landscape of plants and trees, many of which are more than 500 years old. The lush greenery provides a natural habitat for many bird and animal species. More than 2,500 species of aquatic life and more than 1,000 species of plants in the lake have been documented; some are endemic and others are also found in other parts of the world.

Approximately two-thirds of Lake Baikal's shoreline is protected as a nature reserve, but research shows that the lake is polluted by chemical residue from manufacturing runoff. One source of pollutants is the waste dumped from a

pulp and paper plant located on Lake Baikal's southern shore in the city of Baikalsk. It was built in the mid-1950s and, because of a combination of poor law enforcement and lack of environmental regulation, chemical residue from the plant has been released into the lake for many years.

More than 500 rivers, brooks, and streams throughout Russia flow into Lake Baikal bringing runoff from industrial plants, mining sites, and farms. It will take years to restore Lake Baikal to a semblence of its original state.

Lake Baikal is home to thousands of plants and animals. However, these are now being threatened as the lake is being polluted with chemicals.

ENDANGERED WILDLIFE

Only 18 species of seal exist today. While most live in oceans, a few, like the nerpa seal, inhabit freshwater lakes such as Lake Baikal.

The nerpa seal is the smallest of its species. It measures between 47 and 55 inches (1.2 and 1.4 m) long and weighs between 138.9 and 154.3 pounds (63 and 70 kg). It has a life span of 52 to 56 years.

The nerpa seal population has declined due to pollutants in its natural habitat. The seals have suffered from reproductive problems, food

The Eurasian eagle owl is on the endangered species list.

contamination, and lower natural immunity. In addition to these problems much of their shoreline habitat has been lost to land development. The nerpa seal is also hunted for its fur, fat, and meat.

The Eurasian eagle owl is the largest owl in the world. It measures between 23 and 29 inches (58 and 73 cm) in length, has a wing span of 60 to 79 inches (150 to 200 cm), and weighs between 3.5 and 9.3 pounds (1.6 and 4.2 kg).

Mostly brown in color with a white speckled coat, the eagle owl makes its home in the northwestern and central regions of Russia, as well as Siberia. It subsists mostly on a diet of small rodents like mice, squirrels, and hedgehogs, but is capable of killing young deer and other animals of comparable size.

The eagle owl is in danger of extinction because of deforestation, which limits its hunting and nesting areas. Another threat to this giant bird-of-prey is polluted food sources. When toxins get stored in the fat cells of the small rodents on which the bird feeds, it can adversely affect the reproduction rate as well as the life span of the eagle owl.

ENVIRONMENTAL PROTECTION

The following actions are some indications that the Russian government is becoming more environmentally sensitive.

In 1993 the Center for Russian Environmental Policy was founded. Its goal is to educate the public and encourage environment-friendly legislation.

In 1994 the Agreement on Cooperation in the Field of Environmental Protection was renegotiated from its original version in 1972. This

agreement establishes guidelines under which the Russian Federation and the United States can collaborate on environmental issues.

In 2004 President Vladimir Putin promised to ratify the Kyoto Protocol, an international agreement that requires countries to help reduce air pollution. More than 100 countries have already ratified the agreement.

The former Soviet government acknowledged the importance of taking care of the environment. It had set aside more than 160 nature reserves in many biosphere-dependent areas and provided generous funding for scientists to study and support the continuation of various plant and animal species. Unfortunately, this awareness and funding was not extended to the manufacturing and mining industries. After three quarters of a century of generating industrial waste it will take many decades to repair the damage done to the Russian environment. The current government is discussing steps to prevent further damage. At present, succcess depends on the modernization of manufacturing plants and proper industrial residue disposal.

Nature reserves and national parks have been set up in various parts of Russia so that scientists can find ways to ensure that indigenous animals and plants continue to survive in the country.

RUSSIANS

ONE OF RUSSIA'S MOST DISTINCTIVE FEATURES is its multiethnic make-up. This originates from the 14th century, with the founding of the Moscow-centered Russian state. Over the next few centuries, because of the rapid outward expansion in Russia, the people of Siberia, the Volga region, the Far East, and the northern Caucasus became a part of the Russian state, with Moscow as their distant focal point.

Sometimes expansion was achieved peacefully, and sometimes by more forceful means. For example, in the 18th century, acceptance of Russian dominance by 50,000 Kalmyks was achieved through giving them lands between the rivers Volga and Manych in southern Russia, an area they still inhabit today. On the other hand, various tribes in the Caucasus were subdued by military means. Throughout history, Christian peoples came to Russia to flee the expansion of the Islamic Ottoman (Turkish) Empire. Greeks, Bulgarians, and Serbs escaped to Russia, trying to avoid Turkish domination. They were accepted and have made significant contributions to Russian culture.

THE EMPIRE AS AN ETHNIC MOSAIC

In the 19th century, Russia became a colonial power, but unlike England, France, Holland, and Spain, Russia's colonial expansion was not overseas, but involved swallowing up surrounding territories on the European-Asian landmass. Among these territories were the northern part of the Caucasus, Turkestan (including present-day Uzbekistan), Kyrgyzstan, Tajikistan, and Turkmenistan. Some highly developed, complex European cultures, such as Poland and Finland, were also added to the Russian Empire as a result of military conquest.

Catherine II, who was German by birth, invited families from Germany to settle in Russia, and after some time a large German colony formed near Saratov on the Volga River. After the revolution of 1917, this area was transformed into the Volga District German Republic, but the republic broke up during World War II because of the Nazi invasion and has not since been revived.

Opposite: **Russians in traditional costumes.**

Russian children play at a childcare centre in a town north of Moscow.

People from all corners of the empire traveled to the Russian center in order to study and trade and sometimes stayed there, diversifying and enriching Russian life and culture. The Ukrainians, another Slavic people, make up the largest ethnic minority after the Russians and Tatars. Another Slavic people, the Belarusians, make up only a small percentage of the population in the Russian Federation. The process of migration occurred in both directions: many ethnic Russians now live in former Soviet republics such as Ukraine, Belarus, Latvia, Lithuania, and Kazakhstan.

From ancient times, various peoples such as Armenians, Georgians, Kazakhs, Uzbeks, and Azerbaijanis have lived in Russia. Russia also has populations of Gypsies and Jews. For hundreds of years, many rulers and governments tried to make the Gypsies live in permanent settlements, but to no avail. With the creation of an independent Jewish homeland, and with anti-Semitism often a fact of Russian life, many of Russia's Jews have emigrated to Israel.

THE SOVIET CITIZEN

In Soviet Russia, the official policy was to create a new type of citizen who no longer identified with a region or republic, but with the ideology of the party—a "universal" man, dedicated to international socialism. International marriages and migration to other republics were encouraged.

Nowadays, it is evident that this experiment failed. After the breakup of the USSR, national differences quickly surfaced. Nationalism rapidly increased, both in Russia and the former republics of the USSR. The many years of suppression of national identities under the Soviet regime led to

A mother and child from Pskov, one of Russia's oldest cities.

Above: This newly married couple have the typical blue eyes and blonde hair of their Slavic ancestors.

Opposite, top and bottom: Many eastern Siberians have Asian features, in part due to the proximity of Mongolia and China, and in part as a product of the Mongol invasions. The man is from the Yakut region. The girl is a Buryat from Ulan Ude, near Mongolia.

an explosion of nationalist feeling in all parts of the former USSR. Sporadic local wars flared up in many of the distant outposts of the former Soviet Union, particularly in the northern Caucasus, Armenia, Azerbaijan, Moldavia, and Chechnya.

ETHNIC DIVERSITY

There are now more than 100 nationalities living in Russia. According to 2002 statistics, the population is about 145 million, of which about 80 percent are Russians. Moreoever, the Russians are not a homogeneous group but originate from a variety of ethnic backgrounds. For example, Russians living in the north—in Murmansk and Arkhangelsk—or in Siberia, or in the areas bordering Ukraine, are significantly different from each other in their customs and attitudes. Russia's enormous size makes such variations inevitable between people thousands of miles apart.

The modern Russians bearing the closest resemblance to their Slavic ancestors are probably those who live just north of Moscow—the inhabitants of Pskov, Arkhangelsk, and Novgorod. They are fair-haired and blue-eyed, with lean, narrow faces. Asian features are not common in this part of Russia.

SIBERIANS The inhabitants of Siberia represent another type of Russian. Settlers originally came to Siberia in the 17th century to escape the religious reforms under Peter I. They were adherents of the "old faith" and refused to recognize church reforms and modernization; nor would they accept outsiders into their community. They settled in isolated areas, and have managed, to some extent, to maintain to this day the customs, habits, and dress style of traditional Russians.

In the 19th century, many more people from Ukraine, Belarus, and western Russia migrated to Siberia to escape poverty and to gain new land.

Under both the tsars and Communism, Siberia has been used as a place to which political prisoners were sent, and many of Siberia's inhabitants are the descendants of those people.

COSSACKS Cossacks originate from the northern hinterlands of the Black and Caspian seas. The term was applied to peasants who fled from serfdom in Poland, Lithuania, and Muscovy to the Dnieper and Don regions, where they established free, self-governing, military communities. The Russians used the Cossacks to expand their empire eastward and eventually annex Siberia.

A Buryat family. The Buryats mainly live in the mountainous area around Lake Baikal and near the Mongolian border.

TURKS Another significant national group are the Turks. These people live mainly around the lower Volga. They include various ethnic groups, such as the Tatars, Bashkirs, Mordvinians, and Udmurts. They tend to have round faces, slanting cheekbones, narrow eyes, and a short and stocky figure inherited from their ancestors who were nomadic horsemen.

MOUNTAIN PEOPLES Different peoples and nationalities live in the Russian Caucasus. These are the peoples of Dagestan (consisting of dozens of small groups and tribes), the Chechens, Ossetians, Karachayevans, Circassians, Cabardins, and Balkars. Each group has its own individual history and customs. The Ossetians, for example, are the last people to speak the language of the ancient Scythians.

PEOPLES OF THE POLAR NORTH In the ice-bound northern regions of Russia, there live small groups of people generally known as Eskimos. Among them are the Nenets, Chukchis, Komis, Evenks, Yakuts, and Koryaks. These peoples still maintain their ancient languages, which has made them of great interest to philologists and anthropologists.

Some equally small ethnic groups live in the warm south of Asian Russia and in the Far East—the Buryats, Nakasses, Altays, Tuwins, Nganasanes, Yukaghirs, and Tofalars.

POPULATION OF THE RUSSIAN FEDERATION BY ETHNIC GROUPS

Russians	115,889,107	Adyghians/		Gagaus	12,210
Tatars	5,554,601	Adygeys	128,528	Nanais	12,160
Ukrainians	2,942,961	Komi-Permyaks	125,235	Mansis	11,432
Bashkirs	1,673,389	Uzbeks	122,916	Abkhaz	11,366
Chuvashs	1,637,094	Tajiks	120,136	Arabs	10,630
Chechens	1,360,253	Balkars	108,426	Tsakhurs	10,366
Armenian	1,130,491	Greeks	98,727	Pushtuns	9,800
Mordvinians	843,350	Karelians	93,344	Nagaibaks	9,600
Avars	814,473	Turks	92,415	Koryaks	8,743
Belarusian	807,970	Nogays	90,666	Veps	8,240
Kazakhs	653,962	Khakass	75,622	Dolghans	7,261
Udmurts	636,906	Poles	73,001	Romanians	5,308
Azerbaijanians	621,840	Altaics/Altais	67,239	Nivkhs	5,162
Mari	604,298	Circassians	60,517	Indians, Hindi	4,980
Germans	597,212	Lithuanian	45,569	Selkups	4,249
Kabardines	519,958	Nenets	41,302	Serbians	4,156
Ossets/		Abazians (Abaza)	37,942	Tatars (Crimean)	4,131
Ossetians	514,875	Evenks	35,527	Persians	3,821
Darghins	510,156	Chinese	34,577	Hungarians	3,768
Buryats	445,175	Finns	34,050	Udiny	3,721
Yakuts	443,852	Turkmens	33,053	Jews, Mountain	3,394
Kumyks	422,409	Bulgarians	31,965	Turks, Meskhetin	3,257
Ingushs	413,016	Kyrgyz	31,808	Shapsugs	3,231
Lezghins	411,535	Ezedians	31,273	Itelmens	3,180
Komi	293,406	Rutuls	29,929	Bessermyans	3,122
Tuvins	243,442	Khants	28,678	Kumandins	3,114
Jews	229,938	Latvians	28,520	Ulchis	2,913
Georgians	197,934	Aguls	28,297	Checks	2,904
Karachaevtsy	192,182	Estonian	28,113	Uighurs	2,867
Gypsy	182,766	Vietnamese	26,206	Soyots	2,769
Kalmyks	173,996	Kurds	19,607	Mongolians	2,656
Moldovans	172,330	Evens	19,071	All other ethnic	
Laks	156,545	Chukchis	15,767	groups	1,545,707
Koreans	148,556	Shors	13,975		
Tabasarans	131,785	Assyrians	13,649	Total	145,166,731

Source: The All-Russia Population Census 2002

LIFESTYLE

THE LIFESTYLE of the urban and rural populations in Russia differ sharply, as in most other countries in the world. Moscow and St. Petersburg are cosmopolitan, and have many of the same characteristics as cities in Australia, Germany, and the United States. Skyscrapers, however, are fewer and lower, and public transportation, once a source of pride in the USSR, is suffering from declining government subsidies. Road traffic, on the other hand, is increasing rapidly.

CITY LIFE

The clothes worn by urban folk are of an international style—men usually wear European-style jackets, trousers, shirts, and ties, and women wear dresses or blouses with skirts or slacks. Food has also been internationalized—people living in Moscow can eat Chinese, Korean, Indian, French, Italian, and other cuisines.

The work schedule dominates people's daily routine in the cities. On work days, household chores are done when time permits, and most are done over the weekend. The norm in Russia is a five-day work week with two days off, usually Saturday and Sunday. One of the days off is devoted to household affairs and the other is usually spent on entertainment, walks in a local park, or visits to the cinema, theater, museum, parents, or friends. City dwellers pay little attention to the changing seasons, except perhaps to change their attire. In towns, national and religious differences are less noticeable, and everyone spends their work time and holidays side by side, in the same offices and visiting the same restaurants, theaters, and sports stadiums.

Above: **Three students relaxing outside Moscow University.**

Opposite: **Tverskaya Street in Moscow.**

The political liberalization in Russia has led to an explosion in the variety of social activities available in the city. New societies, clubs, and associations have sprung up everywhere, whether political, cultural, artistic, or environmental. In place of the former Communist Party publications there have appeared new and independent newspapers and magazines, such as *Daily Kommersant*—the first daily business newspaper in Russia—and *Delovaya Gazeta*. Unfortunately the increasing costs of newsprint and printing charges have forced some of these publications to close down. Today people rely more on television and radio for their information.

SUMMER ACTIVITIES People from the city usually try to go on vacation in summer to enjoy the warmth of the sun and admire Russia's plethora of flowers, forests, and meadows. It is an interesting paradox that until recently thousands of people, especially the young, have been deserting their native villages for the cities, while at the same time millions of city dwellers have been doing the opposite—trying to get closer to the land by joining gardening societies and *dacha* (DAH-cha—country chalet) cooperatives. About 20 million urban families spend every weekend from April to October tending their gardens—planting vegetables, fruit, and flowers.

Russians of all ages crowd the beaches of the Black Sea coast in the summer months to enjoy the sun before the long, cold winter arrives.

THE ARCTIC NORTH

Children who live in the cold northern regions have their own specific amusements and games. They do not fear the long winter, for this is the time to ski, skate, ride dog sleds, fish through holes cut into the thick ice, and race reindeer.

And what fun it is for children, after spending some time skiing in the freezing cold, to come home and sit by the fire, enjoying thin slices of freshly frozen pink fish meat and drinking sweet, strong tea.

*In summer,
Russian city folk
particularly enjoy
hiking in the
forests and
meadows and
picking berries,
nuts, and mush-
rooms. The child-
ren go swimming
in the rivers and
spend hours tan-
ning in the sun,
trying to absorb as
much sunlight as
they can to last
them through the
next long winter.*

COUNTRY LIFE

Life is quite different in the countryside. Even nowadays, when many urban customs have been introduced into village life and many past traditions have been forgotten, some of the centuries-old customs and rites survive and flourish.

Russia's traditional lifestyle is of a rural nature, since for many centuries most Russians were peasants who worked the land. Village life still depends on the cycle of the seasons. Peasants divide the year's work as follows: sowing and harvesting, grazing the cattle, plowing, hay-making, hunting, collecting fruit, stocking up firewood, and spinning.

The annual folk calendar, a crystallization of the wisdom of many generations of country folk, previously regulated their entire life, from birth to death. These traditions have helped the people to survive despite natural disasters and life under both tsarist and Communist repression, and have given their lives a fixed structure.

CUSTOMS AND FOLKWAYS BASED ON CHRISTIANITY Christianity, which replaced paganism in Russia, added a Christian gloss to the ancient customs, thus making the new religion more understandable to ordinary people. The old Slavic gods were replaced by the Christian saints. The features of Mother-Earth were attributed to the Mother of God. Perun, the god of thunder, became Ilya the Prophet; Veles, the god of cattle, was turned into Saint Vlasy, patron saint of domestic cattle; and so on.

Churches were built in the places where the sacred groves and pagan temples used to stand, and ancient holidays and rites were, in various ways, adapted to Christian feasts. Gradually, the people adopted new customs, and church feasts became the most important celebrations of the year.

NATIONAL COSTUMES

Russian national costumes are a real cultural marvel, for they combine both beauty and utility.

For example, in the north, the Eskimos wear fur clothes where every aspect of dress is thoroughly considered to the smallest detail, and where every lace and string has its role to play in making it easier to put the clothes on, button and unbutton them, so nothing should become unfastened at an improper time. With temperatures as low as –100°F (–73°C), a blunder could cost the Eskimos their lives.

By contrast, there are the beautiful and intricate decorations that adorn the collar, cuffs, and hems of shirts worn by Russian peasants. These beautiful garments originally fulfilled a superstitious function. The ornaments were called *oberegi* (ob-er-EG-ih) from the Russian word *oberegat*, which means "safeguard." The embroidery on the men's shirts was meant to safeguard the wearer against evil spirits.

Folk costumes encapsulate the living history of a nation, and for an expert they are an encyclopedia of folk life; they tell a lot about the history of the nation, its mentality, the climate of the country, and many other things. The diversity of Russian costumes is truly remarkable. The Russians alone have hundreds of costumes, with each *gubernia* (goo-BERN-eea) or province, and sometimes even village, following its own style and fashion. The Buryats have their own costumes, as do the Caucasians and Turks.

Since olden times, the winter months of December, January, and February have been a time when people rested after the hard work done in the fall. That is why weddings, Shrovetide fortune telling, and games in the snow were traditionally held at Christmas, Epiphany, and other winter religious festivals.

An elderly man takes his grandchild out to play in a country park.

The farmer, for example, knew that on Candlemas Day (celebrated on February 2) daylight hours would begin to increase, and that on Semyon's Day, February 3, he was to repair the summer harness for the horses. He also believed that April 8 was the day on which the ice on the river would begin to crack, and on the day of "Alexei, man of God," April 17, the last snows would melt in the fields. On Yegory Veshny's Day, he would drive his cattle to graze and plow his fields.

In this way, the whole year was regulated day by day, and the peasants knew exactly when to pick apples, when to mow oats, and when to celebrate weddings. The life of the peasants was regulated very strictly by the recurring cycle of the four seasons. This tends to make peasants the world over a conservative people who are reluctant to change anything in their lives that has been established through the course of centuries.

CUSTOMS AND FOLKWAYS BASED ON OTHER RELIGIONS The natural cycle has the same role in the lives of the other religious groups living in Russia. The Muslims shape their lives according to the precepts of the Koran, observing holidays and feasts elaborated and adapted by their forefathers. The Buddhists live according to their own rules, as passed on by Gautama Buddha. Although outwardly the customs observed by the

Caucasian mountain peoples, the Buddhists from the Kalmyk steppes, the Siberians living in the *taiga*, or the Chukchis who see nothing but ice and snow all the year round differ, all of them customarily follow the same patterns of life dictated by nature and its seasons.

In the northern wastes of Siberia, it is essential that Yakut children wrap up in thick fur clothing to protect against harsh winter conditions.

EDUCATION

In Russia, education is compulsory and provided by the state. Public school begins at the preschool level, when children are 5 years old. The children play games and are taught to read, write, and count.

Formal education begins at age 6 and continues for nine to 11 years, depending on the schools the child attends. Children go to school six days a week, Monday through Saturday. The school year begins in September and ends in May. It is divided into four terms, with vacations of up to two weeks between the terms.

Russia also has a number of special vocational high schools, where a general education (language, mathematics, physical education, and science) is combined with technical training and some on-the-job experience. In a similar style are the junior colleges (institutes)—places where the students can concentrate on engineering, medical, musical, or art courses, as well as receive a general education. Higher education begins at around age 18 and lasts for five or six years. Again, all higher education is state funded, although students have to attain the appropriate grades to be allowed to continue.

In the 19th century the general emphasis had been on learning for learning's sake. Under Soviet rule, emphasis was on preparing students to perform "socially useful labor." There was a heavy stress on engineering and the sciences needed for industry, and courses in Marxism-Leninism were a mandatory part of the curriculum. Moscow University was perceived as the Harvard of the Soviet Union. Today, a new fact of life is that rich Russians prefer to send their children to private schools and universities abroad, something that was not possible in Soviet times.

Moreover, entrance into new private grammar and high schools is sought after, much for the same reasons as in the United States. There is a perception that they provide a better, well-rounded education; they also serve as a status symbol for the family.

It has been said that during the period 1965–85, serious harm was inflicted on the Russian education system and that young people were prevented from demonstrating the true extent of their abilities by perfunctory instruction and the drive for uniformity.

Current reforms being applied to the system are aimed at making it a more democratic institution, where students play a more active role in their own education and do not study just for the sake of obtaining good grades.

Students using computers in Moscow's Air Training School. Nowadays, it is possible to attend private, fee-paying schools in Russia. There is greater competition for college and university places, so those who get the appropriate grades and are willing to pay fees have an advantage over those who cannot afford the fees.

BIRTH, MARRIAGE, AND DEATH

Traditional rituals connected with birth, coming of age, marriage, and death, are still of an essentially religious nature, despite 70 years of Communism. These rituals, although they differ greatly from religion to religion, are observed for the same reasons. Christians baptize their newborns, while Muslims and Jews circumcise their male infants. These two rites have a similar significance in that they are performed for spiritual purification. Death rites are also similar—relatives and friends pay their respects and wish eternal peace to the deceased.

Funeral rites being performed at a burial in Smolensk.

Under the Communist system, it was usual to have a local Soviet councillor officiate at weddings, filling the role of priest. The practice of exchanging rings and vows was still followed. But with Russia's recent liberalization, more people are opting for a traditional-style wedding conducted by a clergyman of their chosen religion. However, divorce has become a serious problem in Russia. In 1996 the divorce rate in Russia was 65 percent, and shows no sign of declining.

In the 1920s and 1930s, attempts were made to do away with the old rites and rituals, replacing them with new, "socialist" practices. Easter, Christmas, and New Year festivities were abolished and branded as "remnants of the past." Religious feasts were replaced by celebrations of the birthdays of revolutionary leaders and anniversaries of revolutions in various countries. Today, celebrations connected wth revolutionary figures and events are declining in popularity, and old festivals are being restored.

RELIGION

TWO MAJOR WORLD RELIGIONS, Christianity (Orthodoxy) and Islam, have the greatest number of followers in Russia. Small Jewish and Armenian populations and their religions can also be found within the borders of the Russian Federation, as well as Buddhist communities on Russia's southern and eastern borders. Following the Communist authorities' persecution of all religions in Russia for most of this century, many of the churches are currently undergoing a revival in Russia's more liberal climate.

CHRISTIANITY

THE RUSSIAN ORTHODOX CHURCH Christianity, as was noted in previous chapters, came to Russia in the 10th century from Byzantium. Following the East-West schism of 1054, when Christianity was divided into the Orthodox and Catholic religions, Christianity's Eastern branch, the Greek Orthodox Church, prevailed in Russia. The translation of the Greek term "orthodox" means "doctrines that are held as right or true," and hence the official name of the Church in Russia is the Russian Orthodox Church. In the course of five or six centuries, Christianity was introduced into pagan Russia with difficulty and often by force, but on the whole, the process was peaceful, without any massacres or destruction of towns.

Later, the Orthodox Church became so firmly established in the lives of the people that it became an integral part of most Russians' consciousness. After the fall of Constantinople to the Ottoman Empire in the middle of the 15th century, Russia became the chief custodian of the precepts of

Above: **Church banners being carried in a Russian Orthodox procession in St. Petersburg.**

Opposite: **The Cathedral of Saint Basil the Blessed was built between 1554 and 1560. Its construction was commissioned by Ivan the Terrible to commemorate his victory over the Tatars in Kazan and Astrakhan.**

Russian Orthodox clergymen still wear the traditional long, shovel-shaped beard banned by Tsar Peter I.

Orthodoxy and remains so to this day, despite the Communists' attempt to suppress it.

To explain the precepts of Orthodoxy in full is too great a task for this book. We shall only mention that the code of its basic dogmas, the so-called creed, binds every follower of the Orthodox religion to believe in the triune God: God the Father, who created the earth; God the Son (Jesus Christ), who came from heaven to be born of the Virgin Mary, be crucified under Pontius Pilate, and on the third day be resurrected from the dead and ascend into heaven; and God the Holy Spirit, who proceeded from God the Father. This is set forth in clauses one to eight of the creed. Clause nine binds the believer to revere the one holy and apostolic church. Clauses 11 and 12 tell the faithful to expect resurrection from death and eternal life after Judgment Day. The Russian Orthodox Church is headed by the Patriarch of All Russia and does not recognize the Pope.

Some nationalities living in the northern Caucasus, including the northernmost people of northern Ossetia, profess the Orthodox faith, which reached them via Georgia. But many people in this region are Muslims. In the Middle Ages, Christian missionaries preached the new religion among the pagans of northern Russia and Siberia and managed to baptize such groups as the Komis, Permyaks, Maris, and Mordvinians.

In 1990, 18,666 Orthodox communities were officially recorded in the Soviet Union as a whole, most of which were in Russia. The church has regained much of its prosperity and has gained many more adherents.

OTHER CHRISTIAN CHURCHES   The Orthodox faith differs from Catholicism in a number of religious beliefs and details pertaining to rites and rituals. Nevertheless, it is more similar to Catholicism than to Protestantism. In the Russian Federation, Catholicism has a small number of followers, chiefly among Poles and Lithuanians who have settled there.

An Orthodox Jewish man prays in a Moscow synagogue.

The number of Protestant churches is small. There are also various small groups of Evangelists, Seventh-Day Adventists, and Jehovah's Witnesses, whose popularity is growing.

Armenians have been settling in Russia for many centuries. Large Armenian colonies exist in Moscow, St. Petersburg, Rostov-on-Don, Astrakhan, and other large cities. In each of these places, a branch of the Armenian Church was established. Today, functioning Armenian churches have remained in only a few Russian towns. The Armenian Church is also Christian and considered a branch of the Gregorian Church, which, although similar, differs in some aspects of dogma from both Orthodoxy and Catholicism.

JUDAISM

There is a Jewish population of more than 537,000 people in Russia. Jewish practice was suppressed for decades by the Soviet regime, offering little

Women pray in a Moscow mosque.

opportunity for generations of Jews to follow the faith. In the 1990s more and more synagogues were opened as people felt more free to attend them. But it is difficult to give any real figures for synagogue attendance.

ISLAM

The Islamic religion has the second largest number of adherents in Russia. It is professed mainly by peoples living in the Volga region—the Tatars and the Bashkirs—and by some peoples of the Northern Caucasus—Chechens, Ingushes, and Dagestanis. They all belong to the Sunni branch of Islam. There are no local variations of Islamic teachings, and dogmas, customs, and prayers follow exactly those laid down by the Prophet Mohammed.

BUDDHISM

Buddhism, in the form of Lamaism, is the fourth major world religion to have followers in Russia. Its adherents live in three small republics—Buryat (near Lake Baikal), Kalmyk (on the Caspian Sea), and Tuva (on the Mongolian border).

The Russian tsars favored the Buddhists, perhaps because they were drawn to Buddhism's mystical teachings. For example, Empress Elizabeth (the daughter of Peter I) proclaimed freedom to profess Lamaism in Russia in 1740, the 250th anniversary of which was widely celebrated among the Buddhists of Russia in 1990.

Opposite: **The Cathedral of Christ the Saviour in Moscow was built by Alxexander I.**

RELIGIOUS PERSECUTION

Ever since the reforms of Peter I, the Russian Orthodox Church has been dependent upon the state. The clergy received salaries from the state and were considered mere state officials "concerned with religious affairs."

Soon after the 1917 Revolution, by a decree of the Soviet powers, the Church was separated from the state and made independent. Its first act was the restoration of the Orthodox Patriarchship, which had been banned by Tsar Peter. Freedom to profess and practice any religion was allowed, and religious belief was henceforth considered a matter of individual conscience. This progressive step made by the Soviet powers put all religions in Russia on an equal footing.

The new authorities did not maintain their even-handed attitude for long. Atheism became state policy in the 1920s, and this set off a campaign of persecution of the churches and believers. Clergymen of all religions were herded into labor camps and prisons and branded as "parasites of the working people." Churches and temples were closed down, and their decorations—including those that were of a great artistic and cultural value—were either stolen or destroyed. The buildings were blown up or, at best, used as storehouses, workshops, or club houses. It is impossible to say now how many churches, mosques, and synagogues were destroyed during this period. Religious literature was confiscated and destroyed, and reading the Bible was equated with counter-revolutionary activity. People were not allowed to baptize their newborns or to perform funeral rites for their dead.

This state of affairs lasted until 1942–43 when, amidst the heavy casualties of World War II, the state decided to use religion to boost patriotism in support of the war effort. Some churches were opened, and people talked about the need to wage a "sacred war" against the non-Orthodox German aggressor. After the war, persecution of the church was resumed, first under Stalin and then under the more "liberal" Khrushchev. Again, ancient churches were destroyed, icons burned, and believers persecuted. Many churches were turned into museums.

In the 1970s and 1980s, under the pressure of world opinion, the Orthodox Church was allowed to exist, but only if it limited its role to "promoting peace on earth through prayer." In the 1990s, religion was revived in Russia, and the number of followers of different faiths continues to grow. The once confiscated churches, monasteries, and church property have been handed back to the clergy. It has again become a national custom to celebrate religious holidays like Christmas and Easter for Christians, Id-al-Fitr and Id-al-Adha for Muslims, Yom-Kippur for Jews, and Vesak Day for Buddhists, as well as many other festivals.

РЕСТОРАН
РУССКИЙ ДВОРИК

ЧАЙ
ОБѢДЫ.

LANGUAGE

RUSSIANS ACCOUNT FOR FOUR-FIFTHS of the Russian Federation's population, so it is natural that Russian is the most widely spoken language. Although all ethnic groups living in Russia use their own national languages, a knowledge of Russian is something they all have—it is the common language of Russia and the CIS. For example, a Ukrainian would speak Russian to a Buryat.

Before 1991, Russian was the official language for all the republics of the USSR. Russian is also one of the official languages of the United Nations. The Russian language has one of the richest vocabularies in the world. If in the 18th century, lexical enrichment came from France, today the Russian language incorporates many borrowings from English.

Above: **A letter to the United States. The right-hand side of the letter is written in the Cyrillic script. Note that the country, rather than the person's name, is written first.**

Opposite: **A café sign written in Cyrillic script.**

HISTORY OF THE RUSSIAN LANGUAGE

Russian belongs to the Eastern branch of the Slavic language family, which has its origins in Indo-European. In the sixth through 11th centuries a common East Slavic root language developed from the ancient Slavic language common to all Slavs. In subsequent centuries this East Slavic root language diverged into several languages: Russian, Ukrainian, and Belorussian. There also developed two other branches of Slavic: West and South Slavic. Languages that belong to South Slavic are spoken in the former Yugoslavia, Macedonia, and Bulgaria; languages of West Slavic are spoken in Poland, Slovakia, and the Czech Republic. Because of Hungary's proximity to these countries, people mistakenly assume that Hungarian is also a Slavic language; it is not. Hungarian belongs to the Finno-Ugric branch of Uralic.

The linguistic scenario outlined above is complicated by other factors. One of the important influences on the development of Russian arrived in

A man reading the newspaper. Today, the newspapers available in the country include *Argumenti i Fakti* (Arguments and Facts), *Izvestia* (News), *Daily Kommersant*, *Pravda* (Truth), *The Moscow Times*, and *The St. Petersburg Times*.

the church books that reached Kievan Rus through Bulgaria after the acceptance of Christianity by Prince Vladimir. These books were written in what is known as Old Church Slavonic. As a result, Old Church Slavonic became superimposed on the language spoken in Kievan Rus. As Muscovy grew more powerful and important in the 14th to 16th centuries, Great Russian, or simply Russian, developed there. During Peter the Great's reign, the Russian language borrowed many words from Western Europe, particularly scientific, technical, navigational, and administrative terminology.

In the 18th and 19th centuries, the Russian language further developed amid fighting between the supporters of the older language and those of the rising new style that brought the literary, written language closer to the language spoken by the people. A major influence in this debate was Mikhail Lomonosov (1711–65), who wrote the first scholarly grammar of the Russian language, in which words were classified according to "styles"—high, medium, and low.

Major changes to the language came about at the beginning of the 19th century, thanks to the writings of Alexander Pushkin (1799–1837), the father of Russian literature. Pushkin synthesized various levels of language—folk, Old Church Slavic, and words from Western European languages—to create a new literary language. Many consider him the founder of modern Russian and its phonetic, grammatical, and lexical standards. He had as much (if not more) influence on the development of the Russian language as Shakespeare had on English.

Although in the past two centuries the language has changed a lot and the number of borrowed words has increased, Russians still mainly speak the language in which Pushkin wrote his prose and poetry.

THE CYRILLIC ALPHABET

The oldest treasures of written Russian date back to the 11th century. Earlier examples have not been preserved, or are as yet undiscovered. Experts believe that some kind of written language existed before this time. For example, a 10th-century Arabian traveler mentions that he saw some inscriptions and a name on the tomb of a Russian nobleman. However, it is unknown what kind of inscription this was.

The alphabet of all the Slavic languages that is used today, with some minor differences, by Russians, Ukrainians, Belarusians, Serbs, and Bulgarians, was created in the middle of the ninth century by the brothers Cyril and Methodius. They were two monks involved in translating Byzantine church texts (written in Greek) into the Slavic script. This

Alexander Pushkin is considered the creator of a fully developed Russian literary language. To the later classical writers of the 19th century, Pushkin stands as the cornerstone of Russian literature, and is in novelist Maxim Gorky's words, "the beginning of beginnings."

CYRILLIC	TRANSLIT-ERATION	PRONUNCIATION	CYRILLIC	TRANSLIT-ERATION	PRONUNCIATION
А	a	Father	Р	r	ravioli (rolled r)
Б	b	bit	С	s	Soviet
В	v	vote	Т	t	ten
Г	g	goat	У	u	pool
Д	d	dog	Ф	f	fit
Е	ye	yes	Х	kh	Bach
Ё	yo	yoke	Ц	ts	cats
Ж	zh	azure	Ч	ch	cheer
З	z	zero	Ш	sh	shop
И	i	feet	Щ	shch	fresh sheets
Й	y	boy	Ъ	hardens following vowel	
К	k	kit	Ы	y	shrill
Л	l	let	Ь	softens preceding consonant	
М	m	map	Э	e	bed
Н	n	not	Ю	yu	cute
О	o	owe	Я	ya	yacht
П	p	pat			

The Cyrillic alphabet.

alphabet consisted of 30 letters—some borrowed from the Greek alphabet and others specifically invented to convey the sounds of the Slavic languages that did not exist in Greek. Cyril and Methodius were canonized for their great achievement. When Kievan Rus adopted Christianity in the 10th century, it gained not only books from Byzantium written in Greek, but also books from Bulgaria written in the Slavic script—the Cyrillic alphabet of Cyril and Methodius. This alphabet became the basis of the written Russian language. The Cyrillic alphabet was preserved through the course of centuries in both manuscript form and in the first printed books.

Under Tsar Peter I, the so-called civilian script, which was simpler and more convenient for printing, was introduced. This is the script used today.

The Cyrillic alphabet has also been used to create written languages for those peoples of the USSR that before the 1917 Revolution did not have a written language: the nations of the far north, the Bashkirs, the Buryats, the Kabardino-Balkars, the peoples of Dagestan, the Komis, the Maris, the Mordvinians, and the Yakuts of northern Siberia.

NON-SLAVIC LANGUAGES

Apart from Russian, people in Russia also speak languages belonging to other groups, such as Turkic, Finno-Ugric, and Iranian. Much about the history of these languages has intrigued linguists and scholars.

It has been discovered that the people living in the Urals and the Volga region—the Bashkirs, Udmurts, and Maris—speak languages that are very closely related to Hungarian and Finnish. Linguists believe that these peoples were once related and that they migrated together with the Hunnic hordes of the conqueror Atilla during the great movement of nations in the fourth and fifth centuries. They traveled through the expanses of Asia to Europe and partially settled down, reaching the Danube River and Pannonia (a Roman province in central Europe), where they created the Magyar state, now modern Hungary. Some also traveled north and settled in Finland.

Two Russians study movie listings in Moscow. Today, movies from all over the world can be seen in Russian cinemas.

A well-known Chukchi author, Yuri Rytkheu, looks through some children's textbooks and fiction on the Chukchi Peninsula, Russia's easternmost point. These books have been published in the indigenous language of the region.

NAMES

Russian names dating back to pagan times have practically died out. Only a few have remained and today sound more like nicknames. Some of them sound almost incomprehensible to modern Russians, for example, Yermak, Zhdan, Kruchina, Metla, Pervoi, Tomilo, Nezhdana, and Shchap.

After the conversion of Kievan Rus to Christianity, people began to be given new, Christian names. During the first centuries after conversion people had two names—an old pagan one, and a new Christian name given in baptism.

There used to exist what is known as *Svyatsy* (svYA-tzy)—a church calendar where every day was marked with the names of saints or Biblical personages. A newborn child would usually be given one of the names falling on the day of his/her birth or close to it. Usually, these were names borrowed from the Old or New Testament. From these origins, certain names became nationally popular, for example, Ioann (Ivan), Andrei, Pavel, Pyotr, Filipp, Luka, Matfei (Matvey), and Mikhail; plus female names like Maria, Anna, Marfa, Elizaveta, and Tamara.

This list was increased by names taken from the Byzantine Greeks—Feodor, Georgy (Yuri), Konstantin, Nikolai, Vasily, Alexander, Alexei, Lev, Lydia, Irina, Sofya, Taisia, and others, as well as purely Russian names like Boris, Gleb, Svyatoslav, Vladimir, and names borrowed from Scandinavia—Askold, Oleg, and Igor.

Patronymics (a name derived from the given name of the father) are traditional in Russia. If the father's name is Ivan Krylov, then the son's name, for example, will be Pyotr (given) Ivanovich (patronymic) Krylov (family). Likewise, the daughter's name will be, for example, Natalia Ivanovna Krylova. It is common among friends and aquaintances to address each other by both the given name and the patronymic. The given name and the patronymic are always used when addressing one's superiors.

In the post-revolutionary 1920s, it was the fashion to give "revolutionary" names such as Marat, Zhores, Spartak, and Engels. There were also some very strange names reflecting the new social and political realities—Idea, Raketa, Diktatura, Avangard, Elektron, Revoliutsia, and

Traktor! There even appeared some strange-sounding names that were abbreviations: Voenmor (the Russian abbreviation for the navy), Melor (Marx, Engels, and Lenin, the founders of the revolution), and even Dazdraperma (the first syllables of the Communist slogan "Long Live May Day"). After Lenin's death, there appeared many names that were adaptations of his name. For example, Vladlen, Lenina, Vilen, or Ninel. But all these names have long ceased to be anything but a joke.

Today, the most popular names are derived from Greek and other European languages. The only exception is the female name Indira, reflecting Indian prime minister Indira Gandhi's popularity in Russia.

The names of the peoples of the far north are quite original. Some are difficult to pronounce and very complicated: Akhakhanavrak, Kutyakhsiuk, Eketamyn, Yarakvagvig, and Ememkut. These names have clear-cut meanings, much like those traditionally used by Native Americans. Some, like Volna and Groza (wave and thunderstorm), reflect natural phenomena, while others are definitions of human qualities and properties ("he who owns many reindeer" or "one who is not afraid of evil spirits").

A schoolteacher and her class. Nowadays, Russian children are more likely to be given names of a Greek or European origin, such as Ivan, Pyotr, Georgy, Lydia, Nina, or Tamara. Diminutive names are often used when addressing young girls and boys. For example, a girl named Tatyana may also be addressed as Tanya, Tanyusha, or Tanyechka.

ARTS

RUSSIAN ART is justifiably considered a great contribution to world culture. In the course of nine centuries, Russians have produced a number of outstanding works of architecture, painting, music, and literature.

EARLY RUSSIAN ARCHITECTURE AND ART

For many centuries, Russian architectural styles fell into two types: religious architecture, such as churches and monasteries; and civil architecture, including fortresses, palaces, and houses.

RELIGIOUS ARCHITECTURE In Kievan Rus, churches were the first and best stone structures to be built. In 1037 construction began on Saint Sofia's in Kiev. This was Kievan Rus's first stone cathedral and was built by architects who had come from Byzantium.

Gradually, a national type of church developed. It was called a four-pillar church because the vault was supported from the inside by four pillars. A church could have a different number of domes: one (symbol of Jesus Christ), three (symbol of the Trinity), or five (symbol of Jesus Christ and four Apostles). Magnificent 11th- and 12th- century cathedrals have been preserved in Vladimir, Novgorod, and Pskov, as well as in Kiev in Ukraine.

Russian architecture revived after the liberation of Kievan Rus from the Mongols and the establishment of the centralized Moscow state at the beginning of the 15th century. Century after century, splendid cathedrals and monastery buildings appeared inside the Kremlin fortress to symbolize the might and unity of the Russian state. The remarkable Saint Basil's Cathedral in Moscow's Red Square is unequalled in Russian architecture. It was designed by architects Barma and Postnik on Ivan the Terrible's orders to honor the capture of Kazan in 1552. It is a cluster of nine colorful

The Russian sovereigns paid special attention to consolidating and embellishing their capital city, Moscow. The Kremlin—the tsar's residence— was made particularly beautiful. Under Tsar Ivan III, famous architect Aristotle Fioravanti from Italy was commissioned to build the magnificent five-domed Cathedral of the Assumption in the Kremlin.

Opposite: **A colorful array of Russian *matryoshka* (ma-TRYOH-shka) dolls, where one doll nests within another.**

95

tower-like churches, each crowned with a dome, all of which are connected by internal vaulted passages and surrounded by a circular gallery.

FORTRESSES AND MONASTERIES From the Middle Ages, every town was surrounded by a strong wall to protect it against enemy attacks. Mighty fortresses were built, with towers and walls capable of withstanding assaults and long sieges. In the 16th century, the architect Fyodor Kon designed the walls and towers of the White City as well as the defensive structures of the fortress town of Smolensk, at that time one of the most powerful in Europe. Fortresses can still be found in Tula, Novgorod, Pskov, and Astrakhan.

The 11th-century Lavra Monastery in Kiev, Ukraine, was one of the earliest examples of religious architecture in medieval Rus. The word Lavra indicates that it was the principal monastery in the area. The monastery was used as a fortress by Kiev Russians when the Mongols invaded in 1240.

ICONS

The art of icon painting came to Kievan Rus from Byzantium and achieved a very high standard. The icons brought from Constantinople were highly revered and considered sacred in Russia. One of them, *Our Lady of Vladimir* (11th or 12th century), which according to legend was said to have been painted by the Apostle Luke, had been miraculously preserved in Vladimir. It can be seen at the Tretiakov Gallery in Moscow.

An icon is not just an ordinary painting. It is a special type of religious image that the artist imbues with divine energy, so that the image becomes, so to speak, an aspect and expression of God. All icon painting methods are meant to give the image an ethereal quality in order to illustrate a religious idea. Large eyes are a dominating feature in faces depicted on icons, symbolizing the superiority of the spirit over the body. The background is usually golden-colored and painted in abstract, and is also intended to elevate the representatives of God—the saints and martyrs—from everything earthly. Before starting work on an icon, the artist prepared himself through prayer and fasting. It was believed that it was not the artist who was painting the icon, but that divine energy inspired and worked through the artist.

Due to Western European influence, icon painting became secularized in the 17th century, with icons taking on a more earthly and realistic appearance.

The monasteries, too, were encircled by powerful walls and towers. They were sometimes used as fortresses so that during enemy invasions refugees could be sheltered from the fierce assaults and sieges. Particularly well-fortified were Troitse-Sergeeva Lavra Monastery in the Moscow vicinity, which withstood a 24-month siege by Polish soldiers, and the Solovetsky and Kirillo-Belozersky monasteries (both in the north). Many of them have been preserved and draw large numbers of tourists.

17TH- AND 18TH- CENTURY DEVELOPMENTS

In all spheres of life, the 17th and 18th centuries were a time of the breakdown of the old and the establishment of the new in Russia. The most noticeable changes occurred in architecture, with the building of the new capital of St. Petersburg in 1703. The architects invited from Holland, Italy, and Germany built a city that was more European than Russian.

Most of the buildings of Tsar Peter's time were rebuilt in the 18th century, and some have been preserved to this day: the Saints Peter and Paul Cathedral, Peter I's palace in the Summer Garden, and Menshikov's Palace.

During Catherine II's reign, a number of highly gifted architects worked in Russia and their buildings still adorn many Russian towns. One of the most prominent architects was Bartolomeo Rastrelli (1700–71), gifted Florentine architect who came to Russia as a young man. He built many palaces and churches in St. Petersburg and other towns, and created his own school of architecture. Among his works are the Winter Palace and the palaces of Peterhof and Tsarskoye Selo. By lavishly embellishing the palaces, he created grand buildings in the Baroque style, dramatically changing the appearance of Peter's St. Petersburg.

Italian architect Carlo Rossi (1775–1849) contributed to the grandeur of St. Petersburg; he designed the Mikhailovsky Palace (now the Russian Museum) and added the final touches to the Dvortsovaya (Palace) and Senate Squares. In Moscow, he supervised the building of the Main Headquarters and Theatralnaya Street.

PAINTING

European-style portrait painting developed in Russia in the 18th century, replacing icon painting, and realistically portrayed actual people. At first, only the upper classes and gentry were depicted. Ivan Argunov (1729–1802), who was born a peasant but became a famous painter, was one of the first to paint the life and faces of the common people. His most famous portrait, *A Girl in a Head-Band*, depicts a peasant woman.

Realism affirmed itself in the early 1860s through a group of artists led by Ivan Kramskoi. They broke with the officially backed Moscow Academy of Arts and formed an association of artists who worked together and discussed new literature and art. They felt that the Academy was deeply conservative and divorced from the realities of Russian life. In 1879, on the initiative of Kramskoi and several others, the Society for Circulating Art Exhibitions was

Situated in the town of Pushkin near St. Petersburg is the Catherine Palace, named for Tsar Peter I's wife. It was completed in 1723. Peter's daughter Elizabeth ascended the throne in 1742 and decided to use the palace as her summer residence. An extravagant tsarina, she lavished enormous sums of money on the interior decor.

established, independent of the Academy. Its art exhibits were shown not only in Moscow and St. Petersurg but in many other cities of the country. The *peredvizhniki* (pere-DVIZH-neekee), meaning "itinerants" or "wanderers", as member artists became known, depicted peasant life in a realistic style; they also produced many landscapes of the beautiful Russian countryside. Their interest in the often difficult life of the Russian peasants led to a greater awareness, on the part of the Russian intelligentsia, of the social and moral problems facing Russia.

One of the most famous of them was Vasily Perov (1834–82). His paintings present a panorama of Russian life in the second half of the 19th century. There was no subject he considered unworthy of his art—be it poor children pulling a barrel of icy water on a sledge, a village funeral, or a rural religious procession with a drunken priest.

Vasily Vereshchagin (1842–1904) painted many battle scenes, exposing the essential inhumanity of war. His most famous canvas, *The Apotheosis of War*, depicts a huge mountain of skulls—the result of one of the campaigns of the ancient conqueror Tamerlane—and bears the inscription: "To all the conquerors of the past, present, and future." The heroes of folk and epic tales can be seen on the canvases of Victor Vasnetsov (1848–1926). The most famous of them, *The Epic Heroes*, depicts legendary warriors who defended Russia against the Mongol invasion.

One of the most famous Russian artists of the 20th century is Marc Chagall (1887–1985). Forced to leave the Soviet Union due to difficulties with the Communist authorities, he spent much of his time in exile, mainly in France. He was a prolific painter and book illustrator (he illustrated a rendition of Gogol's *Dead Souls*). Many of his works have religious themes.

The work of Alexander Ivanov (1806–58) stands apart from others. In his monumental canvas *Christ Appears to the People* (above), which took a quarter of a century to complete, he set forth his ideas about life, religion, and the desire for freedom.

99

Kazimir Malevich (1878–1935) was one of the great innovators in art and a pioneer of the Russian avant-garde. He is associated with a movement called Suprematism, which concerned, among other things, the use of color to create the illusion of space. One of his most famous paintings is *Black Square* (1923). His art has been exhibited in galleries around the world.

19TH-CENTURY LITERATURE

The 19th century has been called the golden age of Russian art and culture, for it was then that Russia's greatest works were created in literature, painting, and music.

Ilya Repin's painting, *The Cossacks Drafting a Letter to the Turkish Sultan.*

Alexander Pushkin (1799–1837), Russia's most prominent national poet, is considered the father of modern Russian literature. His many works—*Yevgeny Onegin* (1833), a verse novel, *The Tales of Belkin* (1830), a cycle of realistic stories (the first in Russia), the historical drama *Boris Godunov* (1825), and hundreds of poems—are considered treasures of Russian literature. He was on friendly terms with the Decembrists and addressed one of his poems to the exiles in Siberia. In an effort to subdue and win over the famous poet, Tsar Nicholas I appointed him to court service. Tormented by the nobility and persecuted by creditors, he died defending his honor in a duel with a Frenchman. Crowds of people came to his apartment in St. Petersburg to pay their last respects. Pushkin's work represents in embryonic form almost all the literary genres that developed later in the 19th century.

The work of Nikolai Gogol (1809–52) marks another important stage in the development of Russian literature. In his novel *Dead Souls* (1842) as well as in the play *The Inspector-General* (1836), he satirized the vices

ILYA REPIN

The great realist artist Ilya Repin (1844–1930) was closely linked with the ideas of the *peredvizhniki*. Repin excelled in all genres and was an innovator in each. In the 1870s, his best canvas was *The Volga Haulers*. He devoted a whole series of canvases to the revolutionary movement—*The Arrest of a Political Offender, Refusal to Confess,* and *Unexpected Homecoming.* Among Repin's most popular historical paintings were *The Cossacks Drafting a Letter to the Turkish Sultan* and *Ivan the Terrible and His Son Ivan*, the latter depicting the tsar killing his son in a fit of fury. The apex of Repin's accomplishments is the huge ensemble *Meeting of the State Council*, in which a meeting of the country's highest bureaucrats, presided over by the tsar, is presented without romanticism.

specific not only to Russia with its serfdom, but to all of mankind—the ignorance, legalized corruption, greed, and self-interest of the bureaucracies that are part of absolutist, autocratic governments. Gogol was also the first to portray in literature the "little man"—the world of urban commoners, petty officials, paupers, and the destitute. Gogol's story *The Overcoat* (1842) is considered a classic in which the everyday and the fantastic, the real and the unreal, the serious and the comical are brought together to capture the quality of human life.

REALISM By the middle of the 19th century a more realistic style of writing came into prominence. It was characterized by rich and detailed imagery, attention to psychological description, and a deep interest in conveying the private and public lives of people of various social strata.

Ivan Turgenev (1818–83) is highly representative of this style. In *A Sportsman's Sketches* (1852), he realistically portrays life in the Russian countryside. This book was considered to have played an important part in preparing public opinion for the abolition of serfdom. Turgenev was a keen observer of public life and reflected rising political and social questions in his famous novels *Rudin* (1856), *On the Eve* (1860), and *Fathers and Sons* (1862).

The work of Fyodor Dostoyevsky (1821–81) still continues to have an enormous influence on world literature. Unequalled in his gift for psychological penetration, he understood better than anyone the torment

Mikhail Lermontov (1814–41), whose reputation as a lyricist is second only to Pushkin's, became famous after writing his elegy On the Death of the Poet. *It was devoted to Pushkin, for whose death he blamed high society. In his famous novel* A Hero of Our Time *(1840) he describes the typically super-fluous and idle nobleman of Nicholas I's Russia.*

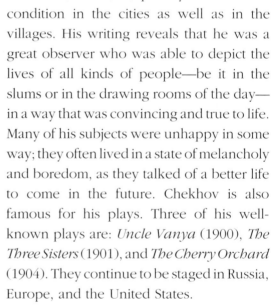

of the "little man," the humiliated, insulted, and oppressed people of tsarist Russia. His novels *Crime and Punishment* (1865–66), *The Brothers Karamazov* (1879–80), and *Possessed* (1871–72) are among the great works of world literature.

The second half of the 19th century saw the rise of another great writer—Leo Tolstoy (1828–1910). In his novels *War and Peace* (1865–69), *Anna Karenina* (1875–77), and *Resurrection* (1899), he vividly reflected life in Russia, with all its complexities and contradictions. Tolstoy was able to bring to life a whole gallery of characters from various social classes. He was a master at capturing the tensions and conflicts that are part of family life.

In his short stories Anton Chekhov (1860–1904) portrayed the human condition in the cities as well as in the villages. His writing reveals that he was a great observer who was able to depict the lives of all kinds of people—be it in the slums or in the drawing rooms of the day—in a way that was convincing and true to life. Many of his subjects were unhappy in some way; they often lived in a state of melancholy and boredom, as they talked of a better life to come in the future. Chekhov is also famous for his plays. Three of his well-known plays are: *Uncle Vanya* (1900), *The Three Sisters* (1901), and *The Cherry Orchard* (1904). They continue to be staged in Russia, Europe, and the United States.

In his stories written at the end of the 19th century, Maxim Gorky (1868–1936) depicted life "in the lower depths." He wrote about

An 1872 portrait by Vasily Perov of the great writer Fyodor Dostoyevsky. Under the harsh dictatorial regime of Tsar Nicholas I, Dostoyevsky was sentenced to death in 1849 for his participation in a radical discussion group. This was later commuted to 10 years imprisonment and exile in Siberia. His novel *The House of the Dead* is a fictionalized account of those experiences.

tramps, beggars, thieves, prostitutes, and the downtrodden, whom he saw as victims of the capitalist economic system. One of his most powerful stories is *Twenty-Six Men and a Girl* (1899) about overworked men in a run-down bakery, and a young girl they befriend. His novel *Mother* (1906) portrays secret revolutionaries working for a new social order. It is considered one of the earliest examples of socialist realism.

MUSIC AND BALLET

MUSIC In the 19th century, Russian musical genius blossomed. Peter Tchaikovsky (1840–93) is probably Russia's greatest composer. His six symphonies, the operas *Yevgeny Onegin, Queen of Spades*, and *Mazepa* (all based on Pushkin's literary works), and the ballets *Swan Lake, Nutcracker*, and *Sleeping Beauty*, represent collectively the summit of Russian musical art. The composer could convey, with tremendous force, the joy, suffering, and conflicts of humankind. Tchaikovsky's works are still popular the world over. The works of other composers—Modest Mussorgsky, Alexander Borodin, and Nikolai Rimsky-Korsakoff—are also acknowledged masterpieces of 19th-century Russian music.

In the 20th century, the traditions of the previous century were continued by the brilliant composers Alexander Skriabin, who reflected the approaching momentous social changes, Sergei Rachmaninoff, who spent much of his life in exile in Europe and the United States, and Igor Stravinsky, who composed the controversial ballet *The Rite of Spring*.

A 1908 photograph of Leo Tolstoy. His autobiographical *A Confession* (1882) gives an account of the spiritual crisis that marked a new direction in his writing.

THE SILVER AGE

The brief period from the beginning of the 20th century to World War I is often called the "silver age" of Russian art, for it rounded off the brilliant culture of the preceding century and witnessed the beginning of its disintegration.

During the reaction and disillusionment after the 1905 Revolution, Fedor Sologub's novels, with their "cult of death," mysticism, and "satanism," and Leonid Andreyev's gloomy, mystical stories became highly fashionable.

However, it was poetry that gained greatest prominence. A brilliant galaxy of poets appeared of various and often mutually hostile trends—the symbolists Valery Bryusov and Andrei Bely and the futurists Vladimir Mayakovsky and David Burlyuk were the best-known. Alexander Blok (1880–1921) was probably the most prominent poet of the epoch, and wrote highly subjective and mystically tinged poetry. His masterpiece is *The Twelve* (1918), which describes Christ in a wreath of white roses, leading revolutionary soldiers patrolling the streets of Petrograd.

BALLET Russian classical ballet is considered perhaps the greatest in the world. There are two main ballet companies in Russia: the Bolshoi in Moscow, and the Kirov in St. Petersburg. Both are world-renowned.

At the beginning of the 20th century, the impressario Sergei Diaghilev (1872–1929) organized extremely successful tours in Europe for his company, Ballets Russes, starring one of the greatest dancers the world has ever seen, Vaslav Nijinsky (1890–1950). Nijinsky gained legendary status for his extraordinary dramatic virtuosity, strength, and featherweight movement.

Russia's greatest female dancer was Anna Pavlova (1881–1931). She also toured with Diaghilev's company and achieved international fame for her discipline, grace, and poetic movement. Rudolf Nureyev (1938–91), who defected to the United States in 1961, was Russia's best-known postwar dancer; a master of fast turns and suspended leaps, he was considered the true heir of Nijinsky.

THE SOVIET PERIOD

The years following the 1917 revolution were a period of great creativity and experimentation in the arts. Various pre-revolutionary groups and schools sought to adapt their art to the goals of the revolution. At the same time, many new writers and artists appeared out of the revolution. They experimented with different styles and techniques as they attempted to not only capture recent history (the revolution and the civil war) but also to describe the new society being built and envisioned in the future. The period up until Stalin's rise to full power in 1929 produced quite a number of brilliant literary works: Mayakovsky's poems, Mikhail Bulgakov's satirical stories, plus Ilya Ehrenburg's *The Life and Adventures of Julio Jurenito*, Yuri Olesha's *Envy*, Alexei Tolstoy's historical and fantastic novels *Aelita*, *Engineer Garin*, and *His Death Ray*, and Mikhail Sholokhov's *And Quiet Flows the Don*.

In music, the young and gifted Sergei Prokofiev, Dimitri Shostakovich, and Aram Khachaturian were composing their first works. Cinema, a new type of art, was rapidly developing. Several Russian films have been shown with great success throughout the world: Sergei Eisenstein's *Battleship Potemkin*, Vsevolod Pudovkin's *Mother*, Nikolai Ekk's *Road to Life*, and the Vasilyev brothers' *Chapayev*.

Under Stalin's oppressive regime in the 1930s, 1940s, and 1950s, the creative arts were put to the service of the state. The task of the Soviet writer and artist was to educate the masses in the spirit of Communist Party ideology, foster allegiance to the state, and glorify its ruler, Stalin. "Socialist realism," which was formally adopted in 1934, was the only acceptable

Russian ballet dancers.

A mosaic on the Moscow subway celebrates Communist brotherhood.

method; it called for portraying life through rosy lenses, placing emphasis on the "paradise on earth" the workers were building. Although not much memorable literature remains from these decades, a number of works have some literary merit, such as Valentin Kataev's *Time, Forward!* (1932), about the construction of Magnitogorsk in the Urals; Konstantin Simonov's World War II novel *Days and Nights* (1944); Viktor Nekrasov's *In the Trenches of Stalingrad* (1946), a novel about the battle for Stalingrad in 1943; and Leonid Leonov's *The Russian Forest* (1953), set on the eve of World War II.

After Stalin's death in 1953, there was a brief period of literary freedom when writers tried to depict the personal lives of their heroes, not just their accomplishments at the workplace. In cinema, *The Cranes are Flying* (1960) and *Ballad of a Soldier* (1960) won world acclaim for their sensitive depiction of the impact of war on private lives. On the other hand, the writer and poet Boris Pasternak found himself more and more persecuted by the authorities. In 1957 he sent his great novel *Dr. Zhivago* to Italy after being unable to publish it in the USSR. Pasternak was awarded the 1958 Nobel Prize in Literature but was "talked out" of attending the ceremonies.

There was another hiatus from government regulation in the early 1960s. The major literary event at the time was the publication of Alexander Solzhenitsyn's *One Day in the Life of Ivan Denisovich* (1962). This novel depicted in great realistic detail the physical and spiritual effort it took to survive one day in one of the Stalinist labor camps in the north. This was the first time the topic of labor camps was written about openly, and the work's publication electrified the nation. A year later, however, at a Moscow art exhibition, Nikita Khrushchev denounced abstract art and literary experimentation in the strongest, crudest terms. Still, young poets such as Yevgeny Evtushenko and Andrei Voznesensky had some of their work published and "village writers" who were critical of city life and morality and found enduring Russian values in the village, produced some good stories and novels. In 1966 Mikhail Bulgakov's masterful novel *The Master and Margarita*, which he wrote in the 1930s, was finally published in 1966, although in censored form. This, too, was a major literary event; the work satirized Soviet artistic life and the materialism of the Moscow elite. The boldest and most unique manuscripts were was smuggled abroad and published there, including Solzhenitsyn's *The Gulag Archipelago* (1973–75).

With the liquidation of censorship amid the new freedoms in post-Soviet Russia, many new writers emerged. The most successful new writer in Russia today is Viktor Pelevin; his stories have been translated into several European languages as well as English. Pelevin's works, such as the collection of stories *The Blue Lantern* (1991) and the novel *Generation P* (1999), revolve around the question of what reality is and can be engaging and entertaining as well as deeply philosophical. There are also greatly admired writers who had begun to write in the 1970s but were only allowed to display the full range of their talent in the 1990s. One such writer is Vladimir Makanin, whose short novel *The Escape Hatch* (1991) provoked heated discussions. It describes two very different worlds, one above ground and another below. Another such writer is Elena Petrushevskaya, whose novel *The Time: Night* (1992) depicts the often harsh, difficult life of women in Russia. In addition, there are several new writers, such as Boris Akunin and Aleksandra Marinina, who write good detective fiction and are widely read. Translations of best-selling authors in the West, such as Stephen King and Danielle Steele, are also widely available and extremely popular.

During the perestroika (pe-re-STROI-ka), a new period of Russian development proclaimed by Mikhail Gorbachev, freedom of speech gradually re-emerged. Books that had lain in writers' desks or archives now began to be published. These included the novel We *by Evgeny Zamyatin, and poems and verse by Pasternak, Osip Mandelstamm, and Anna Akhmatova.*

LEISURE

TYPES OF RECREATION IN RUSSIA do not differ much from those enjoyed in the rest of the world. Russians like to visit their friends and play host to guests. When visiting friends, relatives, or parents, it is customary to bring a simple gift such as a homemade pie, a box of candy, a bottle of wine, or perhaps a toy for the host's children.

PASTIMES

In summer, Russians like to go swimming in their local river or lake, and go mushroom- and berry-picking in the forests. This is easy for villagers, but not for city folk, who have to make a trip to the countryside by train or car. During the Soviet years, recreational centers were built in the villages, containing enough room for a library and movie theater, as well as space for all kinds of other activities, such as singing, dancing, and painting.

Village people can also visit a theater or museum in the nearest town. In Russia, even the smaller towns have their own local museums—often rather good ones—built, as a rule, before the 1917 Revolution by rich patrons of the arts. Often, the rich merchants, after collecting a number of paintings, built a special house for the collection and presented it to their hometown.

The most famous among them was Pavel Tretiakov, a Moscow merchant who owned a large collection of 18th- and 19th- century Russian art. He presented his art collection to the city of Moscow at the end of the last century. Today, the State Tretiakov Gallery is one of the biggest museums in the world.

On the whole, the type of recreation Russians choose depends upon their personal inclinations—some prefer reading a book, others prefer a game of chess, and still others like to tinker with their car over the weekend.

Above: **Two boys playing a game of chess, which is an enormously popular pastime in Russia.**

Opposite: **For some Russians, lying on the grass in the park and spending some time with friends is a pleasurable way to pass the time.**

For the young and athletic Russia there are active pastimes such as country hikes, mountain climbing, and journeys down *taiga* rivers in canoes and kayaks. The "new Russians," or those who have acquired wealth recently, also like to travel to Europe and the United States. For people living in the north of Russia, the most favorite recreation is traveling to the south and the Black Sea coast to the warm sea, to get as much sun as they can to last them through the long northern winter.

In recent times television has become extremely popular, especially among children. Viewers in the main urban centers enjoy access to a number of television and radio stations as well as the Internet. Of course, some regions have more channels than others. Moscow, for example, has a number of channels for educational purposes, and both Moscow and St. Petersburg can receive each other's local television signals.

Television was used as an efficient instrument for testing and analyzing Russia's spirit of openness, known as *glasnost* (GLAS-nost), in the late 1980s. In the 1990s a number of programs focused on recent political and social upheavals in Russia and the rest of the Commonwealth of Independent States. Some parliamentary sessions were also televised. Under Putin independent television stations have been closed, and the government, once more, is moving toward control of television and radio.

Russia's long winters make skating a popular leisure activity.

PHYSICAL ACTIVITY AND SPORTS

Since ancient times Russians have practiced various physical exercises, games, and contests, both as a form of education and as preparation of young Russians for times of war and hardship. In the first half of the 19th century, sports schools, clubs, and societies began to appear in Moscow, St. Petersburg, and Kiev. Regular sports competitions were held in the country, financed by rich landowners, merchants, and aristocrats. In the late 19th century, workers' sports organizations also began to appear in Russia.

In 1896 P. Lesgarf instigated a scientifically based system of physical education called Courses for Physical Training that became the prototype of most sports institutes created in the USSR after the 1917 Revolution. Russia was one of 12 countries in 1894 that decided to revive the Olympic Games and set up the International Olympic Committee.

After the 1917 Revolution, sports and physical training became an integral part of life in the USSR. In the 1930s, fitness programs were instituted to prepare people for work and defense. The benefit of these programs became evident during World War II, when the Russian people were tested to the limits of their endurance by the hardships of war. In Soviet times, in many industries, people briefly interrupted their working day to exercise. Sports were practiced via a wide range of sports clubs, organizations, and groups. This network belonged to the trade unions and was wholly financed by them.

Russia's Svetlana Khorkina is a three-time world gymnastics champion who is well-loved in her home country as well as around the world.

111

Cyclists race through the streets of Moscow.

Under Soviet rule, achievements by the country's sports figures in world competitions were a source of major pride. Such sportsmen were funded by the Soviet government, but managed to retain their "amateur" status for international competitions and the Olympics.

Russia's major sports societies—CSKA (the Central Sports Army Club), Spartak (the trade unions), Lokomotiv (railway workers), and Dinamo (the Interior Ministry)—have major soccer, basketball, and ice-hockey teams with millions of fans in Russia. Baseball is popular, and the first national baseball championships were held in 1989.

Today, there are both voluntary and compulsory sports in Russia. Compulsory exercise programs are a part of the school curriculum, from kindergarten to college level, as well as of the army routine. Sports stars and members of national teams are now paid regular salaries rather than a government stipend for their services. They also sign regular contracts. Over the last few years, a number of Russia's top soccer players have moved to Europe to play for teams there, where players' salaries are more generous than in Russia.

OLYMPICS In 1980 Moscow was the location of the Games of the 22nd Olympiad. The games were marred by the lack of participation of some 60 nations, including the United States, in protest against the Soviet Union's invasion of Afghanistan in December 1979. But a total of 5,179 competitors representing 80 nations did eventually take part. During these games, 36 world, 74 Olympic, and 40 European records were set. Soviet sportsmen set 14 world and 32 Olympic records. The USSR has been a major athletic power in all Olympic events since World War II. Between 1958 and 1988, the USSR won 68 gold medals in track and field events, and 107 gold medals in gymnastics—a traditionally strong sport for Russian athletes. The USSR won another 232 gold medals over the same period in both the winter and summer Olympics. In 1992 Russia's combined team won 54 gold medals. Since then, the Russian Federation has won a total of 110 Olympic gold medals in both the summer and winter games.

Cross-country skiers begin a race near Murmansk in Russia's frozen north.

FESTIVALS

AFTER THE 1917 REVOLUTION, all religious holidays were abolished in the USSR and branded as "vestiges of the past." Together with such Christian holidays as Christmas and Easter, the Islamic Ramadan, and the Jewish Yom Kippur, a ban was also imposed on folk holidays like Shrovetide, New Year, the Tatar Sabantui (Sah-bant-OOEH), and the Islamic Navruz (Nahv-ROOZ). Later, many of these celebrations (for example, Shrovetide) were revived because of their ancient pagan origins. The old holidays were forcibly replaced by new ones that usually celebrated some aspect of the revolution or the new political dogmas. The people accepted some of these holidays and willingly celebrated them. But recent political changes have affected people's attitude towards these festivals.

Opposite: **Father Frost and his granddaughter Snow Maiden are part of the Christmas festivities in Moscow.**

POLITICAL AND PATRIOTIC HOLIDAYS

First among political holidays is National Day (November 7), the anniversary of the 1917 Revolution. Today, the significance and value of the revolution is being reassessed, but the anniversary continues to be marked in Russia, though not celebrated with the same enthusiasm as before in the 1990s.

Under Soviet rule, this event was marked by a number of events—a festive meeting of the party and state leaders in the Bolshoi Theater in Moscow; an anniversary report on the economic situation in the country delivered by a member of the Politburo of the Communist Party Central Committee; a military parade and pro-government demonstration in Moscow's Red Square and in the Dvortsovaya Square in St. Petersburg; and parallel celebrations in all regional capitals. In the evenings, people visited each other and celebrated with a festive meal.

Above: **People celebrate National Day (November 7), the anniversary of the 1917 Revolution, in Moscow's Red Square. Red carnations are carried as a symbol of the revolution.**

115

Another holiday, May 1, the Day of International Solidarity of Working People (known as Labor Day in many countries), was celebrated in much the same manner. Today, the nature of the May Day celebration has changed and it is now called Spring Holiday.

Another public holiday is International Women's Day (March 8), which has a rather interesting history. The celebration was instituted by Clara Zetkin, a veteran German Communist Party leader, as a day of struggle for women's rights. It gradually lost its political content and became Women's Day, on which it was customary for men to present women with flowers and candy, pay them compliments, and attempt to do some of the domestic chores around the house (much like Mother's Day in the United States).

On May 9, tanks take part in the military parade at Moscow's Red Square. This holiday marks Victory Day, the day Berlin was captured in 1945, thus ending World War II.

Victory Day, Russia's most popular patriotic holiday, is celebrated on May 9—the day hostilities ceased in World War II. Military parades are held in Moscow's Red Square, fireworks are exploded over the city, wreaths are laid at the tombs of those who gave their lives fighting for their country, and surviving veterans are honored. A minute's silence is observed in tribute to those who died defending their country in the two world wars.

TRADITIONAL HOLIDAYS

Russia's most popular holidays have an ancient and traditional origin, and many of the celebrations date back to pre-Christian times. They have much in common with festivals celebrated in other parts of Europe.

NEW YEAR New Year is celebrated with much vigor and fanfare in Russia and includes a brightly decorated Christmas tree and the exchange of New Year gifts followed by a hearty dinner. According to tradition, an abundant meal signifies an abundant New Year.

Muscovites celebrate the arrival of the New Year by drinking a toast. It is usual for the Russian head of state to address the nation on television a few minutes before midnight.

Farewell to winter! Butter Week, or Shrovetide, is a celebration of pre-Christian Slavic origin. An effigy of winter is burned to welcome the arrival of spring.

SHROVETIDE   Another popular holiday, Shrovetide (called Butter Week in Russia), occurs the day before Ash Wednesday, the first day of Lent in the Christian calendar. People sit down to a festive meal because it is traditionally the last chance to feast on rich foods before the fasting period of Lent. The highlight of this holiday is the eating of *bliny* (BLEE-nee) or pancakes, a symbol of Yarilo, the ancient pagan sun-god. It is also a time to announce the coming of spring, and a straw figure representing winter is burned at a carnival.

SABANTUI, SURKHARBAN, AND NAVRUZ   Many of Russia's ethnic groups have their own spring holidays that are connected with the completion of the sowing of spring crops. Sabantui is celebrated by the Tatars, and Navruz by other Muslim peoples, but the basic motivation is the same for all—to express joy in anticipation of the coming summer harvest. The name Sabantui is thought to have come from an old nomadic tribe called the Saban. The word later came to mean "plough" and "spring crops." The word tui means celebration. Hence the word Sabantui has come to mean the festival marking the sowing of spring crops. In the days leading up to Sabantui, farmers make little presents for children, such as painted eggs, sweet cookies, and buns. On the day itself, people compete in various

HOLIDAY SONGS

The singing of ditties called *chastushkas* (chast-OO-shkas) was at one time a prominent feature of Russian country festivals and parties. In certain parts of rural Russia they still remain popular. A *chastushka* is a verse of four lines sung in a dance rhythm to the accompaniment of a *balalaika* (ba-la-LAI-ka), a stringed instrument similar to a guitar or Russian accordion.

The song is usually a humorous improvisation on recent local news, in which two performers compete with each other to the general merriment and encouraging applause of the listeners. Both men and women participate.

In modern times, the *chastushka* has moved from rural parties to the variety stage, though it is not as popular as it used to be since it cannot compete with pop music. Yet pointed and clever ditties can still be heard at many rural gatherings.

games and activities such as running, wrestling, the three-legged race, the sack race, and an egg-and-spoon race. All are fiercely contested and popular, and provide those watching with an amusing and exciting spectacle.

The Buryats have a similar holiday, Surkharban (Soor-kah-BAHN), that is celebrated in summer after the crops have been sown. Archery competitions are the main event, as well as wrestling and horse racing. Among the Muslims of Asian Russia, the most important festival is Navruz. It is celebrated particularly by the Uzbeks and Tajiks—the peoples of two former Soviet republics. In the towns and villages, people take to the streets to celebrate the arrival of spring by carrying bouquets of flowers and singing songs to honor the blossoming of nature.

RELIGIOUS HOLIDAYS In the past few years, the once-loved Christian celebrations of Christmas and Easter, and the Islamic holidays of Ramadan and Prophet Mohammed's birthday, have all been revived. They are celebrated much as in any other part of the Christian or Muslim world.

FOOD

RUSSIA IS A MULTIETHNIC COUNTRY where, as one would expect, there is a wide variety of national cuisines, with practically every ethnic group having its own style of cooking and favorite dishes. Several main styles of food can be singled out.

RUSSIAN CUISINE

Today, Russian cuisine enjoys great popularity throughout the world, and some dishes have been included on international restaurant menus.

Russian cuisine has had a long history, stretching back almost 15 centuries. Because of this, the dishes eaten today are quite different from those of the Russians' distant ancestors. Nevertheless, it is precisely from Russia's long history that the main national dishes originate: rye bread, *bliny* (pancakes), pies, *kasha* (KA-sha), which is a kind of gruel made from

Left: **A woman sells pastries in Moscow's Arbat Street. This street is one of Moscow's most popular pedestrian areas and is lined with cosy cafés, souvenir shops, and cultural centers.**

Opposite: **This lady sells ice cream outside the Hermitage Museum in St. Petersburg. Ice cream is sold throughout the year in Russia, even through winter months because many Russians believe that eating it keeps you warm.**

121

Street vendors cook *shashlyk* (shash-LIK), or lamb kebabs, on skewers, providing a nourishing meal in the cold winters. Kebabs are a Caucasian dish from Russia's south-western region.

wheat, rice, or buckwheat, plus other dishes made from vegetables, mushrooms, nuts, and berries.

The Christian Church, which specified a Lenten diet, had a strong influence on Russian cuisine. According to the old church calendar, 192 to 216 days per year were Lenten days (a time when people were allowed to eat only vegetables, mushrooms, and fish, but no meat). Add to this the fact that meat, milk, and eggs were previously something the common people could afford only on major holidays, and it is understandable why Russian traditional cuisine abounds in dishes made from grain (for example, *kasha*), vegetables (in particular cabbage, carrots, potatoes, onions, turnips, and peas), berries, mushrooms, and herbs prepared in a variety of ways, especially boiled, salted, or baked.

The non-Lenten diet—roasted meat, game, and poultry—was more characteristic of the ruling classes and the gentry and was borrowed mainly from Europe, in particular France, Poland, and Germany. The difference

THE INDULGENT TSARS

Here is an interesting excerpt from Alexei Tolstoy's (1817–75) popular historical novel *Prince Serebrennyi* (1874), in which he offers a fictional account of an extravagant feast given by Tsar Ivan the Terrible in the 16th century:

"A great many servants in velvet coats stood before the Tsar, bowed to him, and soon returned, carrying some 200 fried swans on gold trays. Thus began the dinner .... When they had eaten the swans, the servants returned with some 300 fried peacocks, whose fine tail feathers swayed over every dish. The peacocks were followed by fish, chicken meat and cheese pies, *bliny* of all varieties, plus different patties and fritters. While the guests were eating, the servants carried around ladles and goblets of mead .... Although they had spent more than four hours at the table, they were only half way through the meal. The Tsar's cooks really outdid themselves on that day. The huge fish caught in the Northern Seas aroused special amazement. The silver and gold basins, which had to be carried by several people, were hardly big enough for the fish. The hares in noodles were also delicious and the guests missed neither the quails in garlic sauce nor the larks spiced with onions and saffron. But then at a sign from the tablesetters, the salt, pepper and vinegar, as well as the meat and fish dishes, were taken off the tables. The servants brought into the chamber a 180-pound sugar Kremlin and put it on the Tsar's table. It was followed by one hundred gilded and painted trees on which, instead of fruits, were hung cakes made from molasses and honey, as well as other sweetmeats ..."

Such extravagance, which sounds fantastic today, was possible only at the tsar's table. It illustrates that there was much in the Russian cuisine to satisfy any guest!

between the diet of the common people and the ruling classes in Russia was always great until the 20th century. This gap was particularly noticeable in the 15th and 16th centuries, when the aristocrats indulged in extravagant and ostentatious feasts. For example, at banquets given by the tsars, sometimes as many as 200 dishes would be served.

Everyone who sits down to a Russian meal is traditionally served bread first. Russian bread is very special—it is a favorite with all the Slavic peoples—and it is prepared not from ordinary wheat, but from rye. It has a dark color, is soft and spongy in texture, and has a remarkably pleasant flavor. In Russia, wheat bread is also baked, but the rye bread is considered far superior and a real treat for foreigners who have not been introduced to this culinary delight.

This family in St. Petersburg celebrates the New Year with a sumptuous meal and sparklers in their home. Christmas and the New Year are traditional times for Russians to feast.

THE RUSSIAN MEAL

Generally, Russian tables are laid out to include a plate of bread, salt, pepper, and mustard. A guest is first served cold appetizers—cold meat, ham, smoked fish, and vegetables. This also includes the typical Russian salted and marinated tomatoes and cucumbers, plus mushrooms, apples, and of course, wherever possible, red and black caviar. All these typical Russian appetizers are usually washed down with vodka.

Most Russian menus include soups and broths, but the classic opening dish for any meal is *shchi* (sh-chee), a dish that is one thousand years old. This is a vegetable soup in which cabbage (fresh or sour), potatoes, onions, garlic, carrots, roots, and spices are the basic ingredients. *Shchi* has a unique flavor created by the cabbage brine and other ingredients. This flavor is the result of the *shchi* being cooked in an oven. *Shchi* soup is usually served with sour cream. The soup is particularly delicious if eaten with rye bread. The remarkable popularity of this dish is explained by the ready availability of the basic ingredients as well as its good taste.

Ukha (OO-kha) is a hot fish soup prepared from three or four types of fish with potatoes, onions, spices, and herbs added. It is particularly tasty when prepared in the open on the bank of a river where the fish is said to jump into the kettle straight from the water. This kind of soup is referred to as *rybatskaya ukha* (ry-BATS-kaya OO-kha), or fisherman's soup.

Russian main courses are also served hot. This is usually a fish or meat dish, boiled or fried, and garnished with vegetables. Most of these dishes do not differ much from those found in central Europe. Purely Russian main courses are *kasha*, *bliny*, and a variety of meat and cabbage pies.

Kasha is a thick or semiliquid dish made from different cereals, which along with the *shchi* is another thousand-year-old favorite national dish. *Kasha* can be made of peas and ground or whole grains (buckwheat, wheat of different grades, oats, and rice). *Kasha* may be served liquid (as a thin gruel) or thickened, and either sweetened, salted, or unflavored. The method of preparing is very simple and has been tested through the course of centuries; the ingredients are put into boiling water and cooked slowly on a low flame. According to taste, it can be served with sugar, salt, butter, vegetable oil, or gravy.

Bliny is considered the pride of Russian cuisine. This dish has been passed down from the distant pagan past, perhaps from the eighth or ninth century, and resembles pancakes. *Bliny* requires a minimum of flour with a maximum of water or milk, since a very thin batter is needed. Russian *bliny* are soft, porous, and fluffy, and readily absorb all the melted butter, sour cream, jam, or honey that are used as toppings. Needless to say, they are delicious.

Pies are another traditional Russian national dish. Russian pies, or *pirozhki* (pi-ROSH-ki), are comparatively

Matryoshka (dolls) vegetable salad. The eggs are topped with red and black caviar "hair styles" and wrapped in tiny cloth scarfs.

small, elongated, and consist of a filling covered with pastry that is baked in the oven or deep fried in oil. The pastry for the pies may be leavened or unleavened, and the fillings may differ to include cabbage, peas, turnips, carrots, potatoes, spring onions, mushrooms, meat, fish, and even *kasha*. One variety of pie is known as *kulebyaka* (kool-ee-BYA-ka). These are large pies, and the filling (meat, mushrooms, onions, cabbage and boiled eggs, or *kasha*) is spread in layers.

There is another large type of pie that covers the entire baking sheet. These pies are open and not covered with pastry (a bit like a pizza), and are topped with jam. They may have pastry latticework on top.

At the end of the meal, dessert consisting of coffee or tea (traditionally served in a glass) is served with candies or spice-cakes. The latter are made with honey and spices and covered with sweet syrup. Spice-cakes first appeared in Rus sometime around the ninth century, consisting of a mixture of rye flour and honey or the juice of berries. People later began to add spices—cinnamon, cloves, cardamom, and ginger—and this is how the cakes got their name.

Apart from the spice-cakes, a variety of jams and preserves is usually offered with tea. Particularly popular are raspberry, strawberry, apple, and pear jams. Russians often add a spoonful of jam or preserves to their tea instead of using sugar to sweeten the flavor. Many a Russian woman prides herself in making excellent jams and preserves.

Bliny (pancakes) surrounded by a number of possible toppings, including caviar, sour cream, jam, and honey.

DRINKS

The national Russian beverages are *kvass* (k-vhas) and *mors* (morhs). *Kvass* is a beverage that resembles beer, only without the bitterness and alcohol; it is usually made from bread and yeast, although other recipes call for barley, malt, raisins, and other ingredients. *Mors* is made of berry juice diluted with water and slightly fermented.

In times past, there were many meads (alcoholic drinks fermented from honey and water), but they have since disappeared due to the difficulty of making them.

Of the strong liquors, Russian vodka is known the world over. It is a very potent alcoholic drink.

Vodka is the most popular drink for toasting any celebration in Russia.

CUISINE OF THE TATARS AND VOLGA PEOPLES

The dishes of these people are in many respects similar to those of central Asian, and especially Uzbek, cuisine. Typical of this style of cooking are soups of the *shurpa* (shor-PAH) type—made from vegetables, cereals, and fat mutton. *Shurpa* is prepared with a lot of onions, as well as spices—pepper, coriander, and bay leaf. Also very popular is a soup made with *katyk* (kah-TIHK), which is a sour milk made from boiled milk.

Specific to Tatar cuisine are dishes made with horsemeat that has been boiled, dried, and cured. The best-known of the dessert candies is *chak-chak* (chak-chak), which are pieces of pastry boiled in honey.

127

A "cowboy" of the tundra ropes in a reindeer. The people of the northern ranges often eat raw reindeer meat.

CUISINE OF THE CAUCASUS

The food of this region is a mixture of central Asian, Georgian, and Azerbaijani cuisines. From the Turks and central Asians come the unleavened flat cakes, plus mutton dishes and *shurpa* soups. From the Georgians come *shashlyks* and brine cheeses, and from the Azerbaijanis, *khalva* (HAHL-vah), a sweet made from nuts and sunflower seeds. The most typical dish here is *khinkal* (kin-KAHL)— thick noodles boiled with mutton and spices, and *chudu* (choo-DOO)—fried pies of meat, cottage cheese, and onion fillings.

CUISINE OF THE NORTH

This cuisine is the most exotic and unusual. In Arctic conditions, the people have devised a special menu consisting of raw meat and fish. For a long time this was considered a sign of barbarity and savagery, but then it was discovered that the people in northern Russia never suffered from beriberi and other vitamin deficiencies, unlike other Russians. It has also been scientifically proven that their cuisine is ideal for arctic conditions.

Raw food can be of three kinds: fresh meat and fish; the fat and blood of an animal (reindeer, seal, or whale); or both of these two frozen together. *Stroganina* (strog-ah-NIN-ah) is a dish that consists of finely sliced meat or fish that is immediately eaten spiced with salt, roots, and berries. Wind-dried meat and fish is not widely used. Naturally, northern people also like hot dishes—tea, tea with milk, and hot drinks and products made with reindeer milk.

SMALL CABBAGE PIES (PIROZHKI)

This recipe makes 20 to 25 pies.

Ingredients for pastry:
1 pound (450g) flour
1 cup sour cream
2 tablespoons butter or margarine
1 tablespoon sugar
½ teaspoon salt
2 eggs
egg white, beaten lightly with a fork

Ingredients for filling:
1 head of cabbage
2–3 tablespoons butter
3–4 hardboiled eggs, chopped
1–2 tablespoons fresh chopped dill OR
   ½ teaspoon dried dill
1 teaspoon salt
1 teaspoon sugar

Method for making pastry:
Sift the flour. Make a well in the center and add the sour cream, butter or margarine, sugar, and salt. Beat the eggs and quickly mix ingredients into a dough. Shape into a ball and refrigerate the dough for 30 to 40 minutes.

Method for making filling:
Clean and chop the cabbage, scald it in boiling water for 5 minutes, then drain. Pour cold water on it, drain thoroughly again, and put in a pan with melted butter. Sauté for 10 minutes, stirring constantly. Add the chopped hardboiled eggs, dill, salt, and sugar.

Method for making pie:
Roll the dough out to 0.2 inch (0.5 cm) thick. Cut circles in the dough with a glass or cup, and put some filling in the center of each circle. Fold the dough over, then pinch the edges to seal. Glaze the top with beaten egg white. Put the pies on a baking sheet and bake in the oven at 350°F (177°C) for 15 to 20 minutes. To check whether the pies are cooked, pierce one with a toothpick— if the dough does not stick to the toothpick, the pie is ready. The pies should be golden.

BLINY

This recipe serves 2 to 3 people.

3 eggs	½ teaspoon baking soda
3 cups milk	salt and sugar to taste
1 cup flour	2 tablespoons vegetable oil

Mix the eggs and milk. Add the flour, baking soda, and salt to the mixture. Combine thoroughly, making sure that there are no lumps of flour in the mixture. Add a small amount of oil to a non-stick skillet and place on medium heat. When the oil is hot, pour a thin layer of batter evenly into the skillet. Cook till light brown, for about 2 minutes, and flip. Cook the other side till light brown. Serve immediately with your choice of toppings: butter, fruit preserves, sour cream, caviar, cream cheese, salmon, etc.

BEET BORSCHT

This recipe makes 6 servings.

2 beets	1 rib of celery
2 carrots	1 tablespoon parsley flakes
2 onions	salt and pepper to taste
12 cups beef broth	2 cups tomato juice
3 medium white potatoes	1 teaspoon lemon juice
1/4 head cabbage	sour cream and dill to garnish

Use a vegetable peeler to remove the thin outer skin of the beets and carrots. Place the beets and one carrot in a Dutch oven with half of one onion. Add 11 cups of beef broth and bring to a boil. Reduce the heat to medium and skim the foam from the surface. Cook for 20 to 25 minutes till vegetables are soft. Remove the beets and carrot and set aside to cool. Discard the onion. Peel the potatoes and cut them into quarters. Slice the cabbage into strips. Cut up the remaining carrot. Add the potatoes, cabbage, carrot, celery, parsley, salt, pepper, and remaining cup of broth. Cook for 20 minutes. Stir in the tomato juice and cook for another 8 to 10 minutes. Grate or finely chop the cooled beets and carrot. Add to the soup and cook for another 10 minutes. Add the lemon juice and pepper before serving. Serve hot with sour cream and dill.

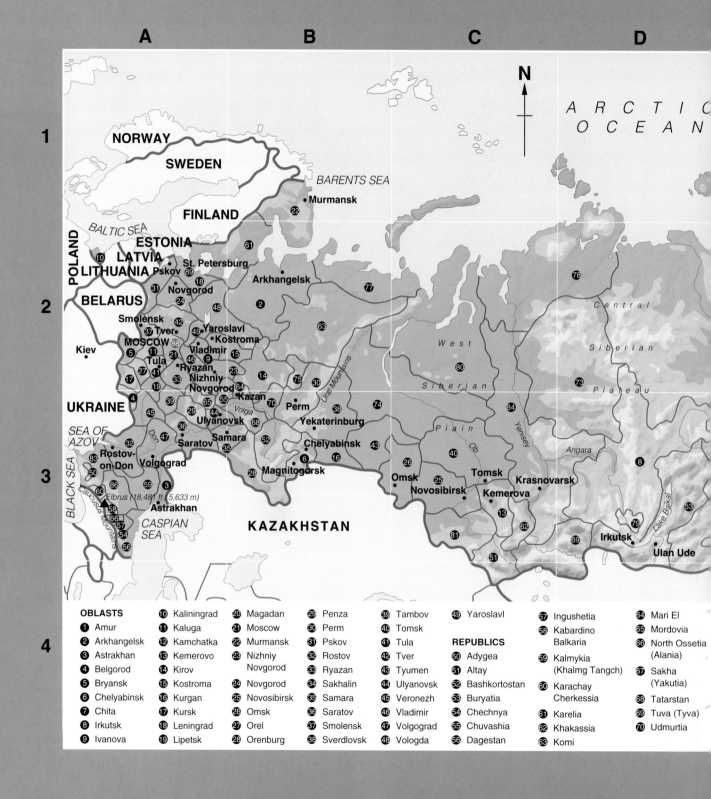

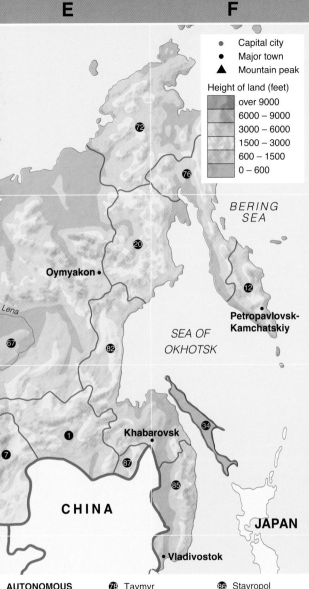

E F

- ● Capital city
- ● Major town
- ▲ Mountain peak

Height of land (feet)
- over 9000
- 6000 – 9000
- 3000 – 6000
- 1500 – 3000
- 600 – 1500
- 0 – 600

72

76

BERING SEA

20

Oymyakon ●

12

Petropavlovsk-Kamchatskiy ●

67

82

SEA OF OKHOTSK

Lena

1

Khabarovsk ●

34

7

87

85

CHINA

● Vladivostok

JAPAN

AUTONOMOUS OKRUGS
- 71 Aginsky Buryat
- 72 Chukchi (Chukotka)
- 73 Evenk
- 74 Khanty Mansi
- 75 Komi Permyak
- 76 Koryakia
- 77 Nenets

- 78 Taymyr
- 79 Ust Orda Buryat
- 80 Yamalo Nenets

KRAYS
- 81 Altay
- 82 Khabarovsk
- 83 Krasnodar
- 84 Krasnoyarsk
- 85 Primorskiy

- 86 Stavropol

AUTONOMOUS OBLAST
- 87 Yevreyskaya

FEDERAL CITIES
- 88 Moscow
- 89 St. Petersburg

MAP OF RUSSIA

Angara (river), C3, D3
Arkhangelsk, B2
Astrakhan, A3

Caucasus Moutains, A3
Central Siberian Plateau, D2
Chelyabinsk, B3

Don (river), A2–A3

Elbrus, A3

Irkutsk, D3

Kazan, B3
Kemerova, C3
Khabarovsk, F3
Kiev, A2
Kostroma, A2
Krasnovarsk, C3

Lake Baikal, D3
Lena (river), D2–D3, E2

Moscow, A2
Murmansk, B1

Nizhniy Novgorod, A2
Novgorod, A2
Novosibirsk, C3

Ob (river), C3
Omsk, C3

Oymyakon, E2

Perm, B3
Petropavlovsk-Kamchatskiy, F2
Pskov, A2

Rostov-on-Don, A3
Ryazan, A2

Samara, A3
Saratov, A3
Smolensk, A2
St. Petersburg, A2

Tomsk, C3
Tula, A2
Tver, A2

Ulan Ude, D3
Ulyanovsk, A3
Ural Mountains, B2

Vladimir, A2
Vladivostok F4
Volga (river), A3, B3
Volgograd, A3

West Siberian Plain, C2–C3

Yarosavl, A2
Yekaterinburg, B3
Yenisey (river), C2–C3, D3

ECONOMIC RUSSIA

Natural Resources	Manufacturing	Agriculture	Services
Coal	Automobiles	Barley	Airport
Fish	Consumer Goods	Oats	Port
Oil/Natural Gas	Hydroelectricity	Potatoes	Tourism
	Steel	Sunflower Seeds	
	Textiles	Wheat	

ABOUT
THE ECONOMY

OVERVIEW
After Russia became independent in 1991 it struggled to build a viable economy. Since 1999 the economy has grown at a steady rate of approximately 6 percent annually. Despite flawed government policies and a 1998 financial crisis that devalued the ruble by 60 percent, the Russian economy shows signs of improving.

GROSS DOMESTIC PRODUCT
$1.282 trillion (2003 est.)
Per capita: $8,900 (2003 est)

GDP SECTORS
Agriculture 5.2 percent, Industry 35.1 percent, Service 59.8 percent (2003)

AGRICULTURAL PRODUCTS
Beef, fruits, grain, milk, sugar beets, sunflower seed, vegetables

INDUSTRIAL PRODUCTS
Chemicals, coal, construction and farming equipment, durables, electric power generators, foodstuff, gas, handicrafts, machine building, oil, textiles

CURRENCY
1 Russian ruble (RUR) = 100 kopecks
USD 1 = RUR 28.78 (October 2004)
Notes: 10, 50, 100, 500, 1000 rubles
Coins: 1, 5, 10, 50 kopecks

NATURAL RESOURCES
Coal, minerals. natural gas, oil, timber

MAJOR TRADE PARTNERS
Belarus, China, France, Germany, Japan, Kazakhstan, Italy, Ukraine, the United States

MAJOR EXPORTS
Chemicals, civilian and military equipment, metals, natural gas, oil, timber, diamonds

MAJOR IMPORTS
Consumer goods, equipment, machinery, meat and poultry, medicine, semifinished metal products, sugar

LABOR FORCE
71.68 million (2003 est.)

LABOR DISTRIBUTION
Agriculture 12.3 percent, industry 22.7 percent, services 65 percent (2002 est.)

UNEMPLOYMENT RATE
8.5 percent (2003 est.)

INFLATION RATE
13.7 percent (2003 est.)

AIRPORTS
2,609 total; 585 with paved runways (2003 est.)

COMMUNICATIONS MEDIA
Telephone: 35.5 million operating main lines;
    17.6 million mobile cellular phones (2002)
Internet: 6 million users (2002)

CULTURAL RUSSIA

Pushkin Festival
Held on the first Sunday in June every year, the Pushkin Festival celebrates the life and works of Russian writer Alexander Pushkin. The festival is held at the Pushkin Estate Museum, located just south of Pskov, and festival goers can expect lectures and poetry readings.

The Hermitage State Museum
One of the greatest and largest museums in the world, the Hermitage in St. Petersburg was once the Winter Palace of Catherine the Great. It is said to house three million exhibits, of which only a fraction can be displayed at any one time.

Mariinsky Theater
This 120-year-old theater in St. Petersburg has played host to the Stars of the White Nights Festival since 1994. In its long history, the theater has seen performances by both the Bolshoi Ballet and the Kirov Opera.

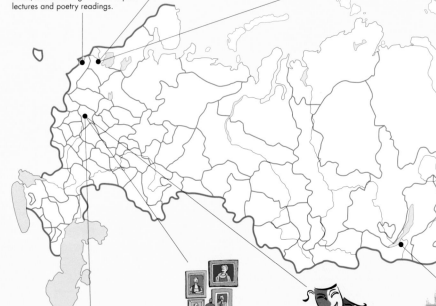

Tretiakov Gallery
Located in Moscow, the Tretiakov contains some of the world's most important Russian paintings. One such painting is "Our Lady of Vladimir," supposedly painted by the apostle Luke.

State Academic Bolshoi Theater
Built in 1776, Moscow's Bolshoi Theater is home to the world-famous Bolshoi Ballet and Bolshoi Opera. It was at this theater that the first production of Tchaikovsky's "Swan Lake" was staged.

Ivolginsk Datsan Temple
This temple in Ulan Ude has the largest Buddhist monastery in Russia and is known as the seat of Buddhism in the country.

The Kremlin
Dating back to the 12th century, the Kremlin in Moscow is known as the seat of the Russian government. The Kremlin is a self-contained city with palaces, cathedrals, armories, and fortresses. Famous sites within the Kremlin include the Red Square, Ivan the Great Belltower, Tsar Cannon and Bell, The Arsenal, Cathedral Square, and the Assumption Cathedral.

Museum "Vladivostok Fortress"
Opened in 1996, this museum honors the Russian navy and commemorates the three centuries that it has helped to protect the country. Vladivostok has a few other museums with naval themes which is apt because the town is Russia's easternmost port and currently the home base of the Russian Pacific Fleet.

ABOUT
THE CULTURE

OFFICIAL NAME
The Russian Federation

NATIONAL FLAG
Three horizontal equal bands with white at the top, red in the middle, and blue at the bottom.

NATIONAL ANTHEM
Anthem of the Russian Federation

CAPITAL
Moscow

OTHER MAJOR CITIES
Chelyabinsk, Irkutsk, Kazan, Khabarovsk, Kostroma, Magnitogorsk, Nizhniy Novgorod, Novgorod, Novosibirsk, Omsk, Perm, Petropavlovsk-Kamchatskiy, Pskov, Ryazan, Samara, Saratov, Smolensk, St. Petersburg, Tomsk, Tver, Ulyanovsk, Vladimir, Vladivostok, Volgograd, Yaroslavl, Yekaterinberg

ADMINISTRATIVE REGIONS
Oblasts: Amur, Arkhangelsk, Astrakhan, Belgorod, Bryansk, Chelyabinsk, Chita, Irkutsk, Ivanova, Kaliningrad, Kaluga, Kamchatka, Kemerovo, Kirov, Kostroma, Kurgan, Kursk, Leningrad, Lipetsk, Magadan, Moscow, Murmansk, Nizhniy Novgorod,

Novgorod, Novosibirsk, Omsk, Orel, Orenburg, Penza, Perm, Pskov, Rostov, Ryazan, Sakhalin, Samara, Saratov, Smolensk, Sverdlovsk, Tambov, Tomsk, Tula, Tver, Tyumen, Ulyanovsk, Veronezh, Vladimir, Volgograd, Vologda, Yaroslavl
Republics: Adygea, Altay, Bashkortostan, Buryatia, Chechnya, Chuvashia, Dagestan, Ingushetia, Kabardino Balkaria, Kalmykia (Khalmg Tangch), Karachay Cherkessia, Karelia, Khakassia, Komi, Mari El, Mordovia, North Ossetia (Alania), Sakha (Yakutia), Tatarstan, Tuva (Tyva), Udmurtia
Autonomous Okrugs: Aginsky Buryat, Chukchi (Chukotka), Evenk, Khanty Mansi, Komi Permyak, Koryakia, Nenets, Taymyr, Ust Orda Buryat, Yamalo Nenets
Krays: Altay, Khabarovsk, Krasnodar, Krasnoyarsk, Primorskiy, Stavropol
Autonomous Oblast: Yevreyskaya
Federal Cities: Moscow, St. Petersburg

POPULATION
143,782,338 (2004 est.)

LIFE EXPECTANCY AT BIRTH
66.39 years (2003 est.)

INFANT MORTALITY RATE
16.96 deaths per 1,000 live births (2004 est.)

ETHNIC GROUPS
Bashkir, Belarusian, Chuvash, Moldavian, Russian, Tatar, Ukrainian

LITERACY RATE
99.6 percent

TIME LINE

IN RUSSIA	IN THE WORLD

1200 B.C.
Cimmerians settle in the area now known as Ukraine

753 B.C.
Rome is founded.

116–17 B.C.
The Roman Empire reaches its greatest extent, under Emperor Trajan (98–17).

A.D. 800
Eastern Slavic tribes settle in various regions of Russia.

A.D. 600
Height of Mayan civilization.

A.D. 988
Grand Prince Vladimir I converts to Christianity and the Eastern Orthodox Church.

1000
The Chinese perfect gunpowder and begin to use it in warfare.

1240
Mongols rule Russia.

1547
Ivan IV—Ivan the Terrible—crowned first czar and extends his power across Russia.

1530
Beginning of trans-Atlantic slave trade organized by the Portuguese in Africa.

1558–1603
Reign of Elizabeth I of England

1620
Pilgrims sail the *Mayflower* to America.

1682
Peter the Great becomes czar and begins modernizing Russia.

1776
U.S. Declaration of Independence

1789–1799
The French Revolution

1825
The Decembrists stage a revolt in St. Petersburg. The revolt fails.

1861
The U.S. Civil War begins.

1869
The Suez Canal is opened.

1903
The Russian Social Democratic Labor Party splits into two groups—the Bolsheviks and the Mensheviks.

IN RUSSIA	IN THE WORLD
1917 Revolutionaries overthrow the Russian government.	**1914** World War I begins.
1922 The Union of Soviet Socialist Republic (USSR) is formed.	
1930 Joseph Stalin begins the Great Purge.	**1939** World War II begins.
	1945 The United States drops atomic bombs on Hiroshima and Nagasaki.
1948 The Soviet Union cuts off contact with the Western world starting the Cold War.	**1949** The North Atlantic Treaty Organization (NATO) is formed.
	1957 The Russians launch Sputnik.
	1966–1969 The Chinese Cultural Revolution
	1986 Nuclear power disaster at Chernobyl in Ukraine
1990 Mikhail S. Gorbachev elected as president of the Soviet Union.	
1991 The USSR collapses and President Gorbachev resigns. Boris Yeltsin is later elected president.	**1991** Break-up of the Soviet Union
	1997 Hong Kong is returned to China.
2000 Vladimir Putin elected president.	**2001** Terrorists crash planes in New York, Washington, D.C., and Pennsylvania.
2002 Russia joins the North Atlantic Treaty Organization (NATO).	**2003** War in Iraq

GLOSSARY

Cyrillic alphabet
A written system developed in the ninth century for Slavic peoples of the Eastern Orthodox faith.

bliny (BLEE-ny)
A light, porous, fluffy pancake that combines the the minimum amount of flour with the maximum amount of water or milk.

Duma (DOO-ma)
The state assembly or council that was first initiated as a result of the failed 1905 Revolution. The *Duma* was a state assembly that constituted the state legislature from 1906 until its dissolution in 1917.

glasnost (GLAS-nost)
Literally means "openness." Former USSR president Mikhail Gorbachev's declared public policy of openly discussing economic and political realities.

kasha (KA-sha)
A semiliquid dish made from a variety of cereals.

kremlin
A fortress in medieval Russian cities. The Moscow Kremlin is used as the seat of Russian government. The term "Kremlin" is often used to signify the Russian government itself.

Oprichnina (ah-PRICH-ni-na)
A policy of terror under Ivan IV. Ivan divided his territory into two domains, one to be administered by traditional institutions, and the other—referred to as oprichinina—to be ruled by him personally.

perestroika (pe-re-STROI-ka)
Literally means "rebuilding" or "remaking." The program of political and economic reform in the USSR initiated by Mikhail Gorbachev in 1986.

pirozhki (pi-ROSH-ki)
A comparatively small elongated pie with filling that is covered with pastry and baked in the oven or deep fried in oil.

serfdom
A modified form of slavery whereby peasants were bound by oath to an hereditary plot of land and to a landowner. The landowner, in effect, owned the peasants and could buy and sell them as he pleased, or volunteer them for army service.

steppe
An extensive plain, especially one without trees. Grass, however, can grow extremely tall. Found in the South and East European and West and Southwest Asian parts of Russia.

taiga (TAI-ga)
Coniferous evergreen forests of subarctic lands covering vast tracts of Russia, especially in Siberia.

tundra
One of the vast, nearly level, treeless plains of the arctic regions of europe and Asia.

Zemstvo (ZYEMST-vo)
Elected rural councils first established in 1864 to provide social and economic services.

FURTHER INFORMATION

BOOKS

Figes, Orlando. *Natasha's Dance: A Cultural History of Russia*. New York: Picador, 2003.

Hirschmann, Kris. *The Deepest Lake (Extreme Places)*. California: KidHaven Press, 2002.

Lincoln, W. Bruce. *Between Heaven and Hell: The Story of a Thousand Years of Artistic Life in Russia*. New York: Viking 1998.

Massey, Suzanne. *Land of the Firebird*. New York: Simon and Schuster, 1982.

Maus, Derek, and Derek C. Maus. *History of the Nations: Russia*. California: Greenhaven Press, 2003.

Murrell, Kathleen Berton. *Eyewitness Books Russia*. New York: Alfred A. Knopf, 1998.

Nickles, Greg. *Russia: the Culture*. New York: Crabtree Publishing Company, 2000.

Nickles, Greg. *Russia: the Land*. New York: Crabtree Publishing Company, 2000.

Nickles, Greg. *Russia: the Peoples*. New York: Crabtree Publishing Company, 2000.

Ransome, Arthur and Simon Galkin. *Favorite Russian Fairy Tales*. New York: Dover Publications, 1995.

Simon, Richmond. *Lonely Planet: Russia & Belarus*. Victoria, Australia: Lonely Planet Publications, 2003.

WEBSITES

Central Intelligence Agency World Factbook (select "Russia" from the country list). www.cia/gov/cia/publications/factbook

Embassy of the Russian Federation in Washington D.C., USA. www.russianembassy.org

Russian Legacy. www.russianlegacy.com

Presiden of Russia. president.kremlin.ru/eng/

U.S. Consulate at Vladivostok, Russia. www.vladivostok-usconsulate.ru

WayToRussia.Net. www.waytorussia.net

The World Bank Russia Country Office. www.worldbank.org.ru

MUSIC

Bering Strait. *Bering Strait*. Nashville: Universal South Records, 2003.

St. Petersburg Balalaika Ensemble. *Music of Russia*. Intersound Records, 1996.

Stars of St. Petersburg. *Balalaika: Russia's Most Beautiful Songs*. New York: Arc Music, 1996.

Various Artists. Rough Guide to the Music of Russia. World Music Network, 2002.

VIDEOS

Face of Russia, Vols. 1–3. Home Vision Entertainment, 1998.

Globe Trekker: Russia—Moscow, St. Petersburg and Murmansk. 555 Productions, 2002.

Russia, Land of the Tsars, Vols. 1–4. A&E Home Video, 2003.

BIBLIOGRAPHY

American Chamber of Commerce in Russia. amcham.ru

Burckhardt, Ann L. *The People of Russia and Their Food*. Minnesota: Capstone Press, 1996.

CIA World Factbook on Russia. www.cia.gov/cia/publications/factbook/geos/rs.html

EIN News: Russia Today. www.einnews.com/russia

Encyclopedia Britannica. Illinois: Encyclopedia Britannica, Inc., 2004.

Information Please Online. www.infoplease.com

International Herald Tribune Online. iht.com

Lands and Peoples. Vol 4. New York: Grolier Educational Publishing Inc., 2001.

Kort, Michael G. *The Handbook of the Former Soviet Union*. Connecticut: The Millbrook Press, 1997.

Murrell, Kathleen Berton. *Eyewitness Books Russia*. New York: Alfred A. Knopf, 1998.

Plotkin, Gregory and Rita Plotkin. *Cooking the Russian Way*. Minnesota: Lerner Publications Company, 2003.

Pravda Russian Newspapers Online. english.pravda.ru/

Radio Free Europe/Radio Liberty. www.rferl.org

Rogers, Stillman D. *Russia: Enchantment of the World*. New York: Children's Press, 2002.

Simon, Richmond. *Lonely Planet: Russia & Belarus*. Victoria, Australia: Lonely Planet Publications, 2003.

Schultze, Sydney. *Culture and Customs of Russia*. Connecticut: Greenwood Press, 2000.

SpaceDaily: Your Portal to Space. spacedaily.com

The All Russia Population Census. www,perepis2002.ru

Turner, Barry (ed). *The Statesman's Yearbook 2003: The Politics, Cultures, and Ecnomies of the World*. Hampshire, England: Palgrave MacMillan, 2002.

World Book Encyclopedia Online. www.worldbookonline.com

INDEX